21ST CENTURY
CENTURY
COMMUNICATION
LISTENING, SPEAKING, AND CRITICAL THINKING

TEACHERS GUIDE

1

Australia · Brazil · Mexico · Singapore · United Kingdom · United States

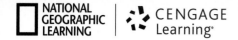

21st Century Communication: Listening, Speaking, and Critical Thinking
Teacher's Guide 1

Publisher: Sherrise Roehr

Executive Editor: Laura Le Dréan

Associate Development Editor: Lisl Trowbridge

Director of Global Marketing: Ian Martin

Product Marketing Manager: Anders Bylund

Sr. Director, Production: Michael Burggren

Manager, Production: Daisy Sosa

Content Project Manager: Mark Rzeszutek

Manufacturing Planner: Mary Beth Hennebury

Interior Design: Brenda Carmichael

Compositor: MPS Limited

For product information and technology assistance, contact us at
Cengage Learning Customer & Sales Support, cengage.com/contact

For permission to use material from this text or product, submit all requests online at **cengage.com/permissions**
Further permissions questions can be emailed to
permissionrequest@cengage.com

ISBN: 978-1-305-95549-3

National Geographic Learning
20 Channel Center Street
Boston, MA 02210
USA

National Geographic Learning, a Cengage Learning Company, has a mission to bring the world to the classroom and the classroom to life. With our English language programs, students learn about their world by experiencing it. Through our partnerships with National Geographic and TED, they develop the language and skills they need to be successful global citizens and leaders.

Locate your local office at **international.cengage.com/region**

Visit National Geographic Learning online at **NGL.cengage.com**
Visit our corporate website at **www.cengage.com**

Printed in the United States of America
Print Number: 03   Print Year: 2017

Table of Contents

Welcome to *21st Century Communication: Listening, Speaking and Critical Thinking.* This four-level series uses powerful ideas from TED Talks to teach learners to think critically and communicate with confidence. Through authentic models of effective communication, students build fluency in the listening and speaking skills needed to achieve academic and personal success.

UNIT OPENER

Each unit begins with an impactful and thought-provoking photograph, **THINK** AND **DISCUSS** questions, and an overview of the unit content.

The **PHOTO** and **UNIT TITLE** introduce the theme of the unit and aim to capture students' attention and curiosity.

TIPS

Ask students questions about the photo and caption.

- What is the first thing that gets your attention, and why?
- What else do you see?
- What interests you, and why?
- What questions do you have as you look at it?
- Do you like the image? Why, or why not?
- What does the caption say?
- What part of the image does it explain?
- Does it answer any of the questions you had about the image?
- Does it help you understand something else about the image? If so, what?

See the unit-by-unit tips and classroom presentation tool for specific teaching information.

21st Century Skill Visual Literacy

Tips for Using Visuals

In addition to the Unit Opener, there are several visuals per unit. Many of them are photos, but they also include infographics and graphic organizers. Using images taps into and builds students' multiple literacies. Being able to read images is an essential 21st century skill. Here are some tips for using the visuals in a unit.

- Have students respond to what they see in the visual; what does it make them think of and why?

- Ask students to explain how a visual helps them understand an exercise or the unit theme.
- Have students cover the caption of an image and then try to guess what the caption is.
- Ask students to explain what they think the message of a visual is, and why.
- Use photos to review and expand target vocabulary by having students describe an image using vocabulary from the current and/or previous unit.

The **THINK** AND **DISCUSS** questions activate students' background knowledge of the topic and help them personalize and relate to the theme. The **OVERVIEW OF CONTENT** allows you and the students to preview the skills they will learn and practice throughout.

TIPS

- Read, or have a student read, the THINK AND DISCUSS questions.
- Have students answer the questions in pairs or small groups before sharing ideas as a whole class.
- If they are not sure how the photo relates to the unit title or theme, read the titles of the Part 1 and Part 2 input and ask them how the image relates to what they will hear in the audio/video input.
- Read, or have a student read, the OVERVIEW OF CONTENT.
- Have the students briefly skim the language skills boxes in the unit. Ask them which of the skills they have studied before, what they already know about them, and what they think they will learn about them in the unit.
- See the unit-by-unit tips and classroom presentation tool for specific teaching information.

PART 1: LISTENING & SPEAKING

PART 1 introduces the listening of the unit. The listening may be one of several genres such as a university lecture, a podcast, an interview, or a student discussion. Where appropriate (and as indicated in unit-by-unit tips), the listening is accompanied by video slides to enhance and clarify the content. The purpose of Part 1 is to prime students for the authentic and inspirational content they will meet in the TED Talk in Part 2.

The **BEFORE YOU LISTEN** section helps students further build schema about the content of the unit. It gets students thinking about and discussing the topic of the listening (top-down processing), and it also familiarizes them with essential vocabulary to understand the listening and do the speaking tasks (bottom-up processing).

TIPS

- For each exercise, read, or have a student read, the directions.
- Elicit from and/or provide to the students any information relevant to the activity (such as definitions of words, examples, relevant background information).
- Put students in pairs or small groups to discuss questions before sharing ideas as a whole class.
- See the unit-by-unit tips and classroom presentation tool for specific teaching information.

21st Century Skill Communicating and Collaborating

Tips for Working in Groups

Students have many opportunities to work in pairs or groups through the built-in COMMUNICATE and COLLABORATE exercises. Additionally, individual exercises can be extended into group exercises by having students share their work. The ability to communicate clearly and to collaborate are essential 21st century skills. Here are some suggestions for arranging diverse pairs and groups, as well as for getting students to work effectively, efficiently, and respectfully during collaborative work throughout the unit.

Arranging Diverse Pairs and Groups

- Have students count off according to how many groups you use. Assign one part of the room to each number, and have the groups convene in their assigned areas. (Alternately, have students "count off" with a set of vocabulary words instead of numbers, and review the meanings of the words with their group members before starting the exercise.)
- Place students of similar levels together, especially when you need to devote more time to working with the lower-level students in a multi-level class.
- Place higher-level students with lower-level students. Tutoring peers reinforces learning for higher-level students, and lower-level students benefit from learning from their peers.

Working in Pairs and Groups

- Have students introduce themselves to anyone they don't know in order to build a positive learning community. This is especially helpful in large classes.
- Tell students what the end requirements are of the pair or group work, so they know what the expectations of each exercise are (e.g., to share a comment they agreed/disagreed with and why).
- Explain to students that they should not only share their own ideas, but should also ask for their classmates' opinions about the topic.
- Assign roles so that everyone participates. The *group leader* keeps the conversation on track. The *time keeper* keeps track of the time. The *recorder* takes notes on the discussion. The *reporter* uses the recorder's notes to report back to the whole class.

VOCABULARY introduces the target vocabulary. Words are selected according to several criteria: frequency, utility, Academic Word List, and CEFR (Common European Framework of Reference for Languages) level. Content-specific words or phrases that are important for comprehension are glossed in *Words in the Lecture*. All of the vocabulary words are on the audio program, so there is always an aural and written model of pronunciation.

TIPS

- Read, or have a student read, the directions before having the students work individually. Then, share answers as a class. Alternately, ask students to compare their work with a partner or small group before sharing as a class.

- Refer students to the online workbook activities for more vocabulary practice.

- See the unit-by-unit tips and classroom presentation tool for specific teaching information.

The VOCABULARY presentation is always followed by a **COMMUNICATE** activity. This is an opportunity for students to show they understand the words and can use them in a familiar context.

TIPS

- Encourage the students to use the words and phrases in bold, which are the targeted vocabulary words.

- Have students work in pairs or small groups before coming back to share as a whole class.

- You may want to go over all of the questions as a class to make sure students understand them, and also provide a model for them.

- See the unit-by-unit tips and classroom presentation tool for specific teaching information.

21st Century Skill Independent Learning

General Tips for Teaching Vocabulary

In *21st Century Communication*, target vocabulary is recycled throughout a unit and across the series giving students multiple opportunities to work with each word. However, in order to truly learn new words, students need to develop vocabulary learning strategies on their own. The ability to work independently and to be self-directed learners are essential 21st century skills. Here are some tips for helping students to build their word knowledge on their own.

- Have students keep a vocabulary log in which they record the unit vocabulary, including definitions, sample sentences, information about pronunciation, and any other important information (i.e., first-language translation, synonyms and antonyms, and collocations). See example in Independent Student Handbook.

- Have students make flash cards. On one side, they should write the word. On the other side, they should draw a four-square grid and distribute the following information into the squares: definition, first-language translation, sample sentence, synonyms.

- Encourage students to study more than just the definitions of new words. In order to have a deep understanding of new vocabulary, students need to understand meaning, as well as connotation, level of formality, word family, pronunciation pattern, and spelling.

The **LISTEN** section in Part 1 provides level-appropriate content that encourages students to think critically and creatively about the theme of the unit. This section includes two comprehension activities: LISTEN FOR MAIN IDEAS and LISTEN FOR DETAILS. It also includes a LISTENING SKILL presentation and practice, and often a NOTE-TAKING SKILL presentation and practice.

TIPS

- Before having the students LISTEN FOR MAIN IDEAS, remind them that the listening is on a topic they have been discussing, so they should keep in mind what they know about the topic as they listen.

- Read, or have a student read, the directions. Explain that when they listen for main ideas, they listen for the most important points, so they shouldn't worry if they don't understand everything.

- Play the audio, or video if available. Have students complete the exercise individually, and then go over the answers as a class. Or, have students check their work with a partner before sharing with the class.

- When the LISTEN FOR MAIN IDEAS exercise is accompanied by a slideshow, ask the students how the visuals helped them understand the main ideas of the listening.

- Before having the students LISTEN FOR DETAILS, explain that for this exercise, they need to listen for specific information. Read, or have a student read the directions and the items in the exercise so that students listen with a purpose.

- Play the audio. Have students complete the exercise individually, and then go over the answers as a class. You could also have students check their work with a partner before sharing with the class.

- See the unit-by-unit tips and classroom presentation tool for specific teaching information.

21st Century Skill Working with Multimedia

General Tips for Using Audiovisuals

An audiovisual slideshow presentation accompanies many of the listening inputs in Part 1 to support student learning. As students will be exposed to multimedia presentations of information at school and work, learning how to understand them and determine their effectiveness are essential 21st century skills. Here are some tips for helping students learn with multimedia in the unit.

- Have students watch the slideshow without the audio first to predict the main ideas of the talk.

- After watching the slideshow with the audio, ask the students how the information on the slides did or did not support their understanding of the listening.

- Have the students work in pairs or small groups to discuss how they might change the slideshow to enhance how effectively it supports the message of the speaker(s).

The **LISTENING SKILL** explicitly teaches a key academic listening skill and provides an example drawn from the listening in Part 1. It gives students a listening strategy to help them better understand the listening in the unit and to develop their overall listening skills. The listening skill may come before or after students LISTEN FOR DETAILS.

TIPS

- Read, or have a student read, the information in the box, and play the audio if included.

- Answer any questions the students may have.

- Read, or have a student read, the directions to the follow-up exercises. Explain to students that they should focus on practicing the specific skill, and not worry if they miss some other information.

- Play the audio. Have students complete the exercises individually, and then go over the answers as a class. Alternately, have students check their work with a partner before sharing with the class.

- See the unit-by-unit tips and classroom presentation tool for specific teaching information.

The **NOTE-TAKING SKILL** explicitly teaches a key note-taking skill to help students build their repertoire of note-taking strategies. It focuses students' attention on strategies for taking notes that they can apply to the listening input. The note-taking skill falls either in Part 1 or in Part 2.

TIPS

- Read, or have a student read, the information in the box, and play the audio or video if included.

- Answer any questions the students may have.

- Read, or have a student read, the directions to the follow-up exercises. Explain to students that they should focus on practicing the specific skill, and not worry if they miss some other information.

- Play the audio. Have students complete the exercises individually, and then go over the answers as a class. You could also have students check their work with a partner before sharing with the class.

- Emphasize that note taking is an individual skill and therefore their notes will likely vary from their classmates'. The key to effective and efficient note taking is for students to develop a comprehensible system that works for them.

- Refer students to the online workbook for more note-taking practice.

- See the unit-by-unit tips and classroom presentation tool for specific teaching information.

The **AFTER YOU LISTEN** section gives students the opportunity to think critically about and discuss the ideas that have been presented. It includes presentation and practice of both a SPEAKING and PRONUNCIATION SKILL. This section also typically includes the unit INFOGRAPHIC, although it may fall in Part 2. Students are asked to interpret the visual and are given the opportunity to personalize. Refer students to the online workbook for more listening practice.

21st Century Skills Critical Thinking

Tips for Teaching Critical Thinking

Students have ample opportunities for critical thinking through built-in THINK CRITICALLY exercises that appear throughout a unit. These exercises ask students to analyze, apply, compare, evaluate, infer, interpret, personalize, reflect, support, and synthesize, among other skills. Thinking critically is an essential 21st century skill. Here are some tips for helping students to think critically throughout a unit.

- Have students think about and share what they liked/didn't like and agreed/disagreed with about the listening prior to completing the exercises.

- Have students respond to the listening from a different perspective. How would someone much older react to the listening? Much younger? Of a different gender? An elected official?

- Have students make text connections. Ask them to relate the listening input and/or follow-up exercises to something in their own lives (text-to-self connection), to another text they have heard, watched, or read (text-to-text connections), and to other real-world events in the past and/or present (text-to-world connections).

The **SPEAKING SKILL** explicitly teaches a key speaking skill to help students express their ideas more effectively. It focuses students' attention on strategies the speakers use in the listening input in Part 1, and gives them opportunities to immediately practice the skill in discussion with classmates.

TIPS

- Read, or have a student read, the information in the box, and play the audio if included.

- Answer any questions the students may have.

- Read, or have a student read, the directions to the follow-up exercises. Explain to students that they should focus on practicing the the specific skill presented.

- Have students complete the exercises individually or in pairs/small groups, as indicated. Then, go over student responses as a class.

- Refer students to the online workbook activities for more speaking practice.

- See the unit-by-unit tips and classroom presentation tool for specific teaching information.

The **PRONUNCIATION SKILL** explicitly teaches a key pronunciation skill to help students better understand the listening in the unit. Additionally, it helps them to be better understood by their listeners when speaking and/or presenting.

TIPS

- Read, or have a student read, the information in the box, and play audio if included.

- Answer any questions the students may have.

- Read, or have a student read, the directions to the follow-up exercises. Explain to students that they should focus on practicing the specific skill presented.

- Have students complete the exercises individually or in pairs/small groups, as indicated. Then, go over student responses as a class.

- Refer students to the online workbook activities for more pronunciation practice.

- See the unit-by-unit tips and classroom presentation tool for specific teaching information.

The **INFOGRAPHIC** is additional content relevant to the theme presented visually in a diagram, chart, graph, or other visual. Students interpret and discuss the information in the visual, deepening their understanding of the topic. It also gives students the opportunity to build the skill of interpreting visual information.

TIPS

- Read, or have a student read, the directions.
- Elicit from and/or provide to the students any information relevant to the exercise (such as explanations of key terms, what's being depicted or compared, what forms of measurement are being used, etc.)
- Haves students work in pairs/small groups, as indicated, before sharing ideas as a whole class.
- See the unit-by-unit tips and classroom presentation tool for specific teaching information.

PART 2: TED TALKS

PART 2 introduces the TED speaker and idea worth spreading. Students watch a carefully curated and sometimes edited TED Talk to inform, inspire, and excite. Using the skills they have learned in Part 1, students are ready to enjoy and be motivated by authentic talks from a wide range of subject areas. Students are encouraged to think critically about the topic and share their ideas about the talk.

The **BEFORE YOU WATCH** section helps students build and activate background knowledge about the TED speaker and the idea worth spreading. The sequence of exercises loosely corresponds to that of Part 1, further encouraging students to use the prior knowledge they established in the first part of the unit.

TIPS

- For each exercise, read or have a student read the directions.
- Elicit from and/or provide to the students any information relevant to the activity (such

as definitions of words, examples, relevant background information).

- Put students in pairs or small groups to discuss questions before sharing ideas as a whole class.
- See the unit-by-unit tips and classroom presentation tool for specific teaching information.

The **VOCABULARY** section in Part 2 introduces the target vocabulary, which is chosen according to the same criteria as in Part 1. All target words are on the audio program so students can hear the correct pronunciation. Content-specific words or phrases that are important for comprehension are glossed in *Words in the Talk*. Refer students to the online workbook for more vocabulary practice. For step-by-step teaching strategies, please refer to the VOCABULARY tips in Part 1.

21st Century Skills Creative Thinking

Tips for Reviewing Vocabulary

In order for students to really learn new vocabulary words, they need repeated exposure to and practice with them. While students have the responsibility to study the words at home, it is beneficial to provide repeated exposure to the words in class, as well. Here are some suggestions for interactive games that can be used throughout the unit to review and get students thinking about words in new ways.

- **BINGO:** Have students draw a three-by-three table in their notebooks. While they do this, write nine vocabulary words (from Part 1 and/ or 2) on the board. Direct students to write one word in each box of their table in any order they want. Then, call out the definitions of the words in random order. The first student to get three words in a row (vertically, horizontally, or diagonally) calls BINGO! For an extra challenge, ask the student to use the three words accurately in sentences.
- **Spin a Story:** Have students work individually, or in pairs/small groups, to describe an image in the unit using vocabulary words from Part 1 and/or 2. For this exercise, the students

should pay particular attention to meaning and use. Set a time limit. The winning student or pair/small group is the one that used the most words correctly.

- **Tic-Tac-Toe:** Draw a three-by-three grid on the board and number each square 1–9. The numbers correspond to nine vocabulary words you want to review. Divide the students into two teams, Team X and Team O, and pick one team to go first. The first team picks a number, and you tell them a word. As a group, they must come up with a sentence in which the word is used and pronounced correctly. If their use and pronunciation of the new word is correct, they get to mark the box with their letter (X or O), and then the other team gets a turn. If their use and/or pronunciation is incorrect, they do not get to mark the box, and the turn moves to the other team. The first group to get three Xs or three Os in a row (vertically, horizontally, or diagonally) wins the game. You may choose to have the students spell the words in this game, too.

The **WATCH** section in Part 2 presents the TED Talk, the culminating listening experience that students have been building to throughout the unit. In addition to watching for MAIN IDEAS and DETAILS, students also complete exercises in which they apply the skills they learned in Part 1 to help them better understand and take notes on the TED Talk.

TIPS

- Before having the students WATCH FOR MAIN IDEAS, remind them that the TED Talk is on a topic they have been discussing, so they should keep in mind what they know about the topic as they watch. Additionally, explain to them that the TED speaker also exemplifies the language skills they have been learning, so they should apply their knowledge of these skills to help them better understand (and take notes on) the TED Talk.

- Read, or have a student read, the directions. Explain that when they watch for main ideas, they watch for the most important points, so they shouldn't worry if they don't understand

everything. This is especially important when listening to authentic English delivered at natural speeds. Remind them that they will watch the talk more than once.

- Play the TED Talk. Have students complete the exercise individually, and then go over the answers as a class. Or, have students check their work with a partner before sharing with the class.

- Before having the students WATCH FOR DETAILS, explain that for this exercise, they need to watch for specific information. Read, or have a student read, the directions and the items in the exercise so that students watch with a purpose.

- Play the TED Talk. Have students complete the exercise individually, and then go over the answers as a class. Alternately, have students check their work with a partner before sharing with the class.

- Before having students complete the remaining exercises, explain to them that some of the exercises are opportunities for them to apply the skills they learned in Part 1.

- Read, or have a student read, the directions. When appropriate, elicit from the students which skills from Part 1 they can apply to each exercise. (Use the classroom presentation tool to display the relevant skill boxes from Part 1.)

- Have students complete the exercises individually, and then go over the answers as a class. You could also have students check their work with a partner before sharing with the class.

- Refer students to the online workbook for more practice watching the talk.

- See the unit-by-unit tips and classroom presentation tool for specific teaching information.

The **AFTER YOU WATCH** section provides opportunities for students to reflect on and think critically about the idea worth spreading in the TED Talk, and to deepen and expand their understanding of the theme of the unit.

TIPS

- Put students in pairs or groups to complete the AFTER YOU WATCH exercises.

- Read, or have a student read, the directions to each exercise. When appropriate, elicit from the students which skills from Part 1 they can apply to each exercise. (Use the classroom presentation tool to display the relevant skill boxes from Part 1.)

- When necessary, ask students to complete part of an exercise individually before sharing with their partners or group members. Then, share ideas as a whole class.

- Refer students to the online workbook for more practice responding to the talk.

- See the unit-by-unit tips and classroom presentation tool for specific teaching information.

EXPAND YOUR VOCABULARY focuses on additional useful phrases and expressions from the TED Talk. Students watch an excerpt from the talk and guess the meaning of the phrase in the Classroom Presentation Tool or in their Online Workbook. While these phrases are not essential to understanding the talk, they will help students expand their vocabulary with everyday expressions.

TIPS

- Read, or have a student read, the directions. Before watching the excerpts, have students share the meanings of any of the words or expressions that they already knew or made a guess at while watching the TED Talk.

- From the Classroom Presentation Tool or DVD, play the video. Do the activity as a class. For individual practice, send the students to their Online Workbook.

- Refer students to the online workbook for more Expand Your Vocabulary practice.

- See the unit-by-unit tips and classroom presentation tool for specific teaching information.

PUT IT TOGETHER gives students the opportunity to consolidate the ideas, language, and skills presented and practiced throughout the unit. Students are first asked to synthesize ideas from Part 1 and Part 2, a task that helps prepare them for the final assignment. The synthesis activity is often accompanied by a graphic organizer to help them organize their ideas visually. The synthesis activity is followed by two main parts: COMMUNICATE and REFLECT.

TIPS

- Read, or have a student read, the directions.

- Elicit from and/or provide to the students any information relevant to the exercise (such as set-up of the graphic organizer, what kinds of information go in each part, etc.)

- Have students work in pairs or small groups, as indicated, and then go over their responses as a class.

- See the unit-by-unit tips and classroom presentation tool for specific teaching information.

The **COMMUNICATE** section features the end-of-unit assignment and provides the necessary support for students to be successful in their presentation.

The end-of-unit **ASSIGNMENT** is a presentation related to the unit theme and idea worth spreading. The presentation takes different forms, from individual and group presentations to role-plays and panel discussions. Students use the ideas from the listening input from Part 1 and the TED Talk from Part 2 as a springboard for talking about their personal connection to the topic. They apply the language skills they have learned to make their presentation more effective.

TIPS

- Read, or have a student read, the assignment. Explain that the assignment is meant to give them a chance to apply the ideas, language, and skills learned in the unit.

- To check students' comprehension of the assignment, ask them to restate in their own words what they need to do (discuss something related to the unit theme), how they need to do it (in the form of a presentation), and why (to demonstrate their ability to talk about the theme of the unit and use the skills learned in the unit).

- See the unit-by-unit tips and classroom presentation tool for specific teaching information.

The **PREPARE** section generally starts with the PRESENTATION SKILL, TED-inspired strategies for effective communication and presentation. These skills are meant to give students confidence and specific tools to use in their presentations. The presentation skill is often exemplified in the TED Talk. PREPARE also introduces students to the evaluation rubric. They will use the rubric to provide feedback to their peers, encouraging them to be active audience members. Teachers may also use this rubric to provide a more formal assessment of student work.

TIPS

- Read, or have a student read, the PRESENTATION SKILL. Play any corresponding video examples.

- Provide any other relevant information or examples.

- Read, or have a student read, the directions to the follow-up exercises. Explain to students that they should practice the PRESENTATION SKILL while preparing for their end-of-unit presentation.

- Have students work individually, or in pairs/small groups as indicated. Play the video if included.

- Go over student responses together as a class.

- Have students read the rubric individually, or together as a class.

- To check that the students understand the rubric, ask them what the categories of assessment are, what the highest score for each category is, and how they can use the rubric as a checklist when preparing for their presentation.

- Refer students to the online workbook for a review of the unit.

- See the unit-by-unit tips and classroom presentation tool for specific teaching information.

When students **PRESENT**, they demonstrate their ability to discuss a topic related to the theme of the unit and the idea worth spreading while incorporating the relevant skills and vocabulary learned from the unit.

TIPS

- Organize the order in which students will present through various methods: Arrange presentations in alphabetical order by students' first or last name (using the earliest letter out of all of the students in a group for group presentations); have students draw numbers to get the order of their presentations; or have students choose from available presentation spots on a sign-up list.

- After all the presentations are complete, have students work in small groups to give feedback to one another on their presentations using the rubric. Then, go over the student responses as a class.

- See the unit-by-unit tips and classroom presentation tool for specific teaching information.

21st Century Tips Interacting Effectively with Others

Tips for Student-to-Student Feedback

Students need to be able to provide and respond to critique in respectful ways both in class and in the workplace. Here are some tips for helping students give and receive feedback on presentations in effective ways.

Giving Feedback

- Have students ask their classmates how they think they did overall before providing feedback.

- Ask students to use "I" instead of or before "you" to emphasize that they are expressing their opinions. For example, they should say, "I think you could improve your introduction," instead of, "You could improve your introduction."

- Explain the sandwich method of providing feedback to the students. First, they should express something that their classmate did well. Next, they present an area for improvement. Then, they sandwich the negative feedback with a comment about another thing their classmate did well.

- Ask students to always provide examples or reasons for their opinions so that their classmates have a clear idea of why they did well, or not so well, in certain areas.

- Have students support their opinions with specific information in the rubric.

Receiving Feedback

- Explain to students that when they receive feedback, they should listen and not feel the need to respond immediately. They should listen to their classmates' opinions, and ask clarifying questions, and then thank their classmates for their feedback.

- Explain to students that they do not need to agree with their classmates' opinions. Ultimately, they decide what feedback to accept and reject. However, it is not necessary to tell their classmates what they plan to do with the feedback.

- Ask students to have an open mind. Their classmates view their presentations from many different perspectives, and their feedback will reflect these various points of view. Feedback may unexpectedly highlight an area of strength or weakness for reasons students may never have considered.

REFLECT provides students with an opportunity to contemplate their progress toward acquiring the skills and vocabulary in the unit before moving on to the next unit.

TIPS

- Read, or have a student read, the directions.

- Explain that they should make an honest self-assessment so they know what they have accomplished and what they still need to improve.

- To encourage students to continue to improve on weaker areas, have them write some learning strategies and goals next to the areas they want to develop.

- See the unit-by-unit tips and classroom presentation tool for specific teaching information.

The classroom presentation tool (CPT) provides a central focus during lessons and a dynamic way to use the student book material. It integrates a variety of teaching resources, including audio, video, and interactive student activities that can easily be used on a computer or Interactive White Board (IWB). Additionally, *21st Century Communication* provides Conversation Starters, Answers, and Skill Checks to support teachers as they start an exercise, work through an exercise, or review skills.

You can play the audio that accompanies activities directly from the Classroom Presentation Tool. Simply mouse over and click on the audio icon, and an audio player will open. Click on Script to view the karaoke-style script. Use the player button to pause, stop, or replay the audio at any time.

You can play the videos of the Part 1 slideshows and Part 2 TED Talks that accompany activities directly from the Classroom Presentation Tool. Simply mouse over and click on the video icon, and the video player will open. Subtitles are available for all videos except the Part 1 slideshows and Expand Your Vocabulary and Presentation Skill videos. Click On or Off to turn the subtitles on or off. Use the player button to pause, stop, or replay the video at any time. If audio and a video slideshow are both available for exercises in Part 1, play the video before doing the interactive activity (described below). Only the audio will be available upon launching the interactive activities.

Interactive activities are available in Part 1, Part 2, and Put It Together for all exercises with discrete answers, such as multiple choice, True/False, and matching questions. Students or teachers can click through these activities to complete an exercise together or to review the answers. Interactive activities provide a more dynamic way to engage with the content of the student book, and a fast

and effective way to relay answers to students. Relevant audio and video accompanies these activities, but only the audio is available with the interactive activities in Part 1. Video accompanies most activities in Part 2.

Conversation Starters are available in Part 1, Part 2, and Put It Together for pair or small group exercises that include, but are not limited to, students communicating their opinions and ideas, predicting and reflecting on content, and personalizing content. They help students start discussions by providing them with a model exchange *before* they start communicating in pairs or small groups. Additionally, they model critical thinking.

Answers are available in Part 1, Part 2, and Put It Together for questions that are more open-ended. These model level-appropriate answers that students can check their own responses against *after* they finish an exercise. Exercises with Answers include, but are not limited to, responding to questions about an image, audio, video, or speaker; interpreting an infographic; taking notes; and synthesizing information.

Skill Checks are available in Part 2 and the beginning of Put It Together for exercises that apply the listening, note-taking, speaking, and pronunciation skills students learned in Part 1. They are images of the relevant skill boxes available to display at point-of-use. The Skill Checks reinforce student learning by reviewing the skills at the moment they are needed. In the final part of Put It Together, no Skill Checks are provided, affording students the opportunity to make the connections themselves.

PART 1

Tips for Saving Water

Listening
Listen for Numbers and Statistics

Note Taking
Use an Outline

Speaking
Give Tips or Suggestions

Pronunciation
Syllable Stress

PART 2

TEDTALKS

Joe Smith
How to use a paper towel

PUT IT TOGETHER

Communicate
Give a Group Presentation

Presentation Skill
Focus Your Topic

UNIT THEME

By providing specific steps people can take to conserve water and paper, Unit 1 explores the importance of individual actions in helping to bring about positive change.

ACADEMIC TRACK

Conservation

UNIT OPENER Time: 5–10 min

Ask guiding questions, such as:

- Where was the picture taken according to the caption? *(It was taken in the Molai Forest, on the island of Majuli in India.)*
- Who is the man? *(He is Jadav Payeng, the man who planted the forest.)*

THINK AND DISCUSS (page 3)

Possible answers:

1. *It means people can do small things in their lives that make big changes in the world.*
2. *A man, Jadav Payeng, is standing in a forest, pointing up at a plant or tree.*
3. *Jadav planted trees on the island of Majuli in India. The trees became the large Molai Forest. The forest saved the island and is the home of several endangered species. Jadav's small personal action had big results in the world.*

PART 1

Tips for Saving Water ▶ **Slideshow available.**

The listening is from an interview on a TV talk show called *Daily Report*. The guest speaks about the importance of water conservation and gives viewers tips for saving water at home. Her message is that small changes in our lives can have a significant impact in the world.

BEFORE YOU LISTEN ◔ Time: 30–40 min

A COMMUNICATE (page 4)

Read the image caption together as a class before students discuss questions in pairs. Check understanding of key concepts:

- What is asparagus? *(a vegetable)*
- What water problems can farmers have? *(too much or too little rain)*
- How can farmers change the way they use water? *(plant different crops that need more or less water; water plants at night when the temperature is cooler)*

B THINK CRITICALLY Predict. (page 4)

Ask students to predict some specific tips that they might hear in the interview. Prompt students by asking:

- What are some ways that water is wasted?
- What are some ways that we can save water?

VOCABULARY

C 🎧 **1.2** (page 5) Audio: 1:41 min

D COMMUNICATE (page 6)

For more practice, go to MyELT.

LISTEN ◖ Time: 30–40 min

E 🎧 **1.3** ▶ **1.1** **LISTEN FOR MAIN IDEAS**
(page 6) Audio: 3:41 min Video: 3:46 min

> **LISTENING SKILL** **Listen for Numbers and Statistics** (page 7)
>
> **EXPANSION** Check students' listening comprehension of numbers by having them write down the following numbers as you say them: 13, 30, 14, 40, 15, 50, 16, 60, 17, 70, 18, 80, 19, 90. Then, write the numbers on the board in pairs (13 and 30, 14 and 40, etc.). Have students work with a partner. Each person secretly writes down one number from each pair on a piece of paper. Partner A then reads his or her numbers and Partner B writes them down. Partner A checks Partner B's work. Then they switch.

F 🎧 **1.4** **LISTEN FOR DETAILS** (page 7)
Audio: 2:08 min

> **NOTE-TAKING SKILL** **Use an Outline** (page 8)
>
> Point out that much less information than what the speaker actually said is included in an outline. Emphasize noting only the most important ideas. Clarify the format used in outlining: Roman numerals for main ideas, capital letters for main details, and Arabic numbers for specific details. Clarify using indentation: main ideas are not indented, main details are indented once, and specific details are indented twice.

G 🎧 **1.5** (page 8) Audio: 2:01 min

Check understanding of how to read and use an outline:

- What is the main idea of the outline? How do you know? *(Saving Water. It's at the top of the outline, has a Roman numeral, and is not indented.)*
- What are the main details? How do you know? *(Why is it crucial to save water?; Tips for saving water at home. They have capital letters and are indented once.)*
- What are the specific details? How do you know? *(Save money; Not enough fresh water; Don't run the water when you brush your teeth; Take shorter showers; Don't eat meat; Fix leaky faucets. They have Arabic numbers and are indented twice.)*

AFTER YOU LISTEN ◖ Time: 20–30 min

H COMMUNICATE (page 8)

I THINK CRITICALLY Interpret an Infographic.
(page 9) 💡

Check understanding of the infographic:

1. What is the infographic showing? *(how much water is used in different parts of an average U.S. home)*
2. How does it show this information? *(by comparing percentages of total water used)*
3. How many liters are in one gallon? How many liters are in 265 gallons? *(1 gallon = 3.79 liters; 265 gallons = 1,003.13 liters)*

For more practice, go to MyELT.

SPEAKING ◖ Time: 40–50 min

> **SPEAKING SKILL** **Give Tips or Suggestions** (page 10)
>
> Explain that the imperative form is more direct, while *You should/shouldn't* and *It's (not) a good idea to* are less direct and, therefore, more polite.

For practice with the imperative, go to MyELT.

J COLLABORATE (page 10) 💡

Have students work in different groups than they did for exercises H and I.

K COMMUNICATE (page 10)

EXPANSION Have students discuss who they would give these tips to in the imperative form, and who they would give them to using *You should/shouldn't* and *It's (not) a good idea to*.

> **PRONUNCIATION SKILL** 🎧 **1.6** Syllable **Stress** (page 10) Audio: 0:19 min
>
> Explain to students that correct syllable stress will increase the comprehensibility of their speech. If appropriate, point out that in some cases, syllable stress changes the form of a word (e.g., in**sult**—verb vs. **in**sult—noun).

L 🎧 **1.7** (page 11) Audio: 0:26 min

M (page 11)

N COMMUNICATE (page 11)

21C SKILL Reason Effectively. Challenge students to explain *why* they think a particular fact is true or false. Ask students what information they used to make each decision.

For more practice, go to MyELT.

PART 2 TEDTALKS

How to use a paper towel

JOE SMITH'S idea worth spreading is that there are very simple steps we can take to reduce our environmental impact—starting with a smarter way to use paper towels.

BEFORE YOU WATCH ◐ Time: 30–40 min

A THINK CRITICALLY Predict. (page 12)

Ask students how using paper towels might be related to conserving water. *(They're both resources we need to conserve.)*

B COMMUNICATE (page 12)

VOCABULARY

C 🎧 **1.8** (pages 13–14) Audio: 1:30 min

D COMMUNICATE (page 14) ☑

Review syllable stress. Ask students to discuss and make a note of how many syllables each word in bold has, and which syllable is stressed.

For more practice, go to MyELT.

WATCH 🕐 Time: 40–50 min

E ▶ 1.2 WATCH FOR MAIN IDEAS (page 15)
Video: 4:15 min

After students have completed the exercise, ask them to discuss with a partner why numbers 1, 3, and 4 are incorrect. *(1 is a detail; 3 it too broad; 4 is not discussed.)*

F THINK CRITICALLY Reflect. (page 15)

> learn**more** (page 15) Ask students: How common are paper towels in your country? Are they more common at home or in public places?

G ▶ 1.3 WATCH FOR DETAILS (page 16)
Video: 2:04 min ☑

After viewing the video, ask students how the numbers help support the speaker's idea worth spreading. *(The first number shows the large number of paper towels Americans use each year. The second shows how much paper we could save if we used one less paper towel per day. The third shows the large number of recycled paper towels people usually use at one time.)*

H THINK CRITICALLY Reflect. (page 17)

I ▶ 1.4 EXPAND YOUR VOCABULARY (page 17) Video: 2:02 min

Check understanding of the vocabulary words:

- What other things can be *kicked out* of machines? *(candy, chips, soda, water)*
- What are some examples of other things that are *way too big* that may be negatively impacting our environment? *(food portions, automobiles, factories)*

- What will you remember *for the rest of your life? (important advice; the first time you...)*
- What is another thing that might not seem important, but is really *no small thing? (smiling, being polite, daily habits)*

J WATCH MORE (page 17)

For more practice, go to MyELT.

AFTER YOU WATCH ⏱ Time: 10–20 min

K THINK CRITICALLY Interpret an Infographic. (page 18) 💡

Check understanding of the infographic:

- What is the connection between paper waste and digital media? *(Digital media reduces paper waste.)*
- What different methods does the infographic use to represent how much paper is wasted? *(pie charts, numbers, and images of envelopes, stacks of paper, trees, and a baseball stadium)*

PUT IT TOGETHER ⏱ Time: 10–20 min

A THINK CRITICALLY Synthesize. (page 19) 💡

B THINK CRITICALLY Personalize. (page 19) ☑ 👥

Ask for some examples of resources that people can try to conserve in order to help the environment and write them on the board. Have students work in small groups to share tips or suggestions for conserving the resources. Then have volunteers share their ideas with the whole class.

COMMUNICATE ⏱ Time: 40–50 min + presentations

ASSIGNMENT Give a Group Presentation about tips for helping the environment. (page 19)

ALTERNATE ASSIGNMENT Have students work individually.

- For individual presentations, assign students different resources. Explain that individual presentations can include more personal connections, such as country- or culture-specific ways of wasting a resource and tips for conserving it.

PREPARE

PRESENTATION SKILL Focus Your Topic (page 20)

C –G (pages 20–21)

PRESENT

H (page 21)

I THINK CRITICALLY Evaluate. (page 21)

EXPANSION Ask students to write a short journal entry about what they did well in their presentation and at least one specific goal they have for making the next presentation even stronger.

REFLECT BOX (page 21) Have students work in small groups to review vocabulary use. Each group should go around in a circle, taking turns using each word in a sentence until all words have been used.

For more practice, go to MyELT.

THINK AND DISCUSS (page 3)

1. Answers will vary. (E.g., people can do small things to make big changes in the world) **2.** Answers will vary. (E.g., a man standing in a forest pointing up at something) **3.** Answers will vary. (E.g., Jadav planted trees on an island in India. The trees became the large Molai Forest. The forest saved the island and is the home of several endangered species. Jadav's small action had big results.)

PART 1

Tips for Saving Water

A COMMUNICATE (page 4)

1. Answers will vary. (E.g., picking an asparagus plant; he is a farmer) **2.** Answers will vary. (E.g., some people have too much rain; other people do not have enough water) **3.** Answers will vary.

B THINK CRITICALLY Predict. (page 4)

Answers will vary.

C VOCABULARY (page 5)

1. crucial **2.** resources **3.** huge **4.** on average **5.** conserve **6.** requires **7.** cut **8.** leak **9.** wastes **10.** statistics

D COMMUNICATE (page 6)

Answers will vary.

E LISTEN FOR MAIN IDEAS (page 6)

1. c **2.** b, c **3.** b

F LISTEN FOR DETAILS (page 7)

Segment 1

1. 70, 2 **2.** 7.5 billion **3.** 9 billion

Segment 2

4. 1,799 **5.** 3,000; 13

G (page 8)

B. Tips for saving water at home

1. Don't run the <u>water</u> when you <u>brush your teeth</u> **2.** Take <u>shorter showers</u> **3.** Don't eat <u>meat</u> **4.** Fix <u>leaky faucets</u>

H COMMUNICATE (page 8)

1. Answers will vary. (E.g., to save money, and to conserve the world's supply of fresh water) **2.** Answers will vary. **3.** Answers will vary.

I THINK CRITICALLY Interpret an Infographic. (page 9)

1. 265 **2.** 29% **3.** The toilet **4.** Answers will vary. (E.g., swimming pools, coffee makers, fish tanks) **5.** Answers will vary. (E.g., People who live in a hot, dry country will need to use more water outdoors if they have a garden. People who live in a country with a lot of rain will not need to use much water outdoors.)

J COLLABORATE (page 10)

Answers will vary. For example:

Fix / Replace leaky faucets / toilets   Don't run / Turn off the water while shaving / brushing teeth   Don't take long showers   Don't take baths   Don't water the garden in the hottest part of the day   Don't flush the toilet every time   Cut your shower time   Fill the dishwasher / washing machine before you run it

K COMMUNICATE (page 10)

Answers will vary.

L (page 11)

con<u>ser</u>ving <u>enough</u> statistics <u>leak</u>y

per<u>cent</u> popul<u>at</u>ion sug<u>gest</u>ions <u>wast</u>ed

M (page 11)

See answers for exercise L.

N COMMUNICATE (page 11)

1. False. The correct number is about 69%. **2.** True. **3.** True. **4.** False. Fish need oxygen to live. If the water they are swimming in does not have enough oxygen, they can drown. **5.** False. NASA has discovered water in the form of ice on the moon. **6.** False. It takes 18 gallons. **7.** True. **8.** False. The opposite is true. **9.** True. **10.** False. The world record for holding one's breath underwater is 22 minutes.

PART 2 TEDTALKS

How to use a paper towel

A THINK CRITICALLY Predict. (page 12)

Answers will vary. (E.g., how to use a paper towel to reduce our environmental impact)

B COMMUNICATE (page 12)

Answers will vary.

C VOCABULARY (pages 13–14)

1. c **2.** b **3.** b **4.** a **5.** b
6. c **7.** a **8.** a **9.** c **10.** b

D COMMUNICATE (page 14)

Answers will vary.

E WATCH FOR MAIN IDEAS (page 15)

2.

F THINK CRITICALLY Reflect. (page 15)

1. Answers will vary. (E.g., printer paper, newspaper, food packaging) **2.** Answers will vary. (E.g., at work, on the bus or train, at the grocery store) **3.** Answers will vary. (E.g., hand dryers)

G WATCH FOR DETAILS (page 16)

Segment 1

1. b **2.** a **3.** c **4.** a

Segment 2

1. You should follow two steps to use a paper towel correctly.

  A. Shake **B.** Fold

H THINK CRITICALLY Reflect. (page 17)

1. Answers will vary. (E.g., He wants to show us how large the number is.) **2.** Answers will vary. (E.g., Paper comes from trees. When you waste paper, you waste trees, and trees are an important natural resource.) **3.** Answers will vary. (E.g., dry your hands completely by following his two-step method: shake and fold) **4.** Answers will vary. (E.g., he is joking that he will give another talk on how to use less toilet paper. This is funny because it's not something people usually give a talk about.) **5.** Answers will vary.

I EXPAND YOUR VOCABULARY (page 17)

1. b **2.** a **3.** a **4.** b

K THINK CRITICALLY Interpret an Infographic. (page 18)

1. digital media **2.** 30 **3.** 44% of unwanted mail is tossed into a landfill unopened. Answers to the other parts of this question will vary. **4.** Answers will vary. (E.g., newspapers, magazines, catalogs) **5.** Answers will vary. (E.g., To help us understand where paper comes from and how many trees are needed to make it.) **6.** Answers will vary.

PUT IT TOGETHER

A THINK CRITICALLY Synthesize. (page 19)

	INTERVIEW: TIPS FOR SAVING WATER	TED TALK: HOW TO USE A PAPER TOWEL
1. Resource	Water	Paper
2. What are some ways we use the resource?	To drink, brush our teeth, take a shower, produce meat	To dry our hands
3. How do we waste the resource?	By running the water when we brush our teeth, taking long showers, eating a lot of meat, having leaky faucets	By using too many
4. Tips for saving the resource	Don't run the water when you brush your teeth. Take shorter showers. Don't eat meat, or eat less meat. Fix leaky faucets.	Shake your hands before you dry them with a paper towel. Fold one paper towel to dry your hands completely.

B THINK CRITICALLY Personalize. (page 19)

Answers will vary. (E.g., gas)

C (page 20)

Answers will vary. (e.g., electricity, gasoline, natural gas, glass, metal, paper, water)

D—REFLECT (pages 20–21)

Answers will vary.

UNIT 2 Connecting to Nature

UNIT THEME

These days, many people connect to each other through technology, and no longer connect to nature in the same way as in the past. Unit 2 looks at how photography allows us to connect with nature in a meaningful way.

ACADEMIC TRACK

Photography

UNIT OPENER Time: 5–10 min

Ask guiding questions, such as:

- What is happening? *(Two women are sitting in a jeep with two cheetahs standing on it. One woman is about to take a picture of the cheetah standing on the roof.)*
- How would you feel in her situation? *(afraid, excited, etc.)*

THINK AND DISCUSS (page 23)

Possible answers:

1. *It means feeling part of the natural world around you.*
2. *The photo shows people connecting to nature by being so close to wild cheetahs.*

PART 1

Photos from a Safari ▶ **Slideshow available.**

The listening is a conversation between a man who has just come back from a photo safari and a female colleague. He tells her why he went on safari and shows her some of his favorite photos taken on the trip. He also describes the animals you can see on safari and what it is like to experience wildlife firsthand.

BEFORE YOU LISTEN   Time: 25–35 min

A COMMUNICATE (page 24) 💡

B 🎧 **1.9** **THINK CRITICALLY** **Predict.** (page 24) Audio: 0:31 min 💡

Ask students to predict some specific reasons why the man went on the safari. *(He likes to take pictures, travel, connect to nature, etc.)*

VOCABULARY

C **1.10** (page 25) Audio: 1:29 min

D COMMUNICATE (page 26)

For more practice, go to MyELT.

LISTEN 🕐 Time: 30–40 min

E 🎧 **1.11** ▶ **1.5** **LISTEN FOR MAIN IDEAS**
(pages 26–27) Audio: 4:01 min Video: 3:55 min

WORDS IN THE CONVERSATION

Check students' understanding of *poaching*:

- Why do people *poach*? *(for food, money, adventure, etc.)*
- What can be done to prevent *poaching*? *(create more wildlife reservations, educate people about the negative consequences, fine people who buy or sell animal parts or products)*

F 🎧 **1.11** **LISTEN FOR DETAILS** (page 27)
Audio: 4:01 min

LISTENING SKILL 🎧 **1.12** **Recognize a Speaker's Tone and Feeling** (page 27)
Audio: 0:28 min

Ask students what other words or expressions show other emotions such as surprise, anger, or sadness.

G 🎧 **1.13** (page 28) Audio: 1:36 min

AFTER YOU LISTEN 🕐 Time: 5–10 min

H **THINK CRITICALLY** Reflect. (page 28) 👥

For more practice, go to MyELT.

SPEAKING 🕐 Time: 45–55 min

SPEAKING SKILL **Use Descriptive Language** (page 28)

Point out that descriptive adjectives are often one word that comes before a noun to describe that noun. Descriptive details can be found in other parts of the sentence and often contain more than one word. Tell students that varying the types of descriptions can make a story more interesting and realistic.

For practice with *be* and descriptive adjectives, go to MyELT.

I 🎧 **1.14** (page 29) Audio: 0:55 min

Encourage students to use both descriptive adjectives and descriptive details.

J COMMUNICATE (page 29)

PRONUNCIATION SKILL 🎧 **1.15** **Thought Groups and Pausing** (page 29) Audio: 0:14 min

K 🎧 **1.16** (pages 29–30) Audio: 1:18 min

L 🎧 **1.16** (page 30) Audio: 1:18 min

M (page 30)

EXPANSION Ask students to repeat the sentences twice: first focusing on thought groups, and second focusing on tone to express different feelings. Encourage students to try out different tones and expressions to show feelings such as happiness, sadness, excitement, anger, and boredom. Have their partners try to guess what feelings their partner intended.

N **THINK CRITICALLY** Interpret an Infographic. (pages 30–31) 💡

Check understanding of the infographic:

- What is the infographic showing? *(a comparison of how endangered different types of animals are)*
- How does it show this information? *(by using different colors for different degrees of endangeredness, and animals facing different directions for increasing or decreasing populations.)*

21C SKILL Make Inferences. Ask students to think of possible reasons why specific animals are in more danger than others:

- What reasons can you think of that would cause elephants to be vulnerable? *(People poach them for their tusks.)*
- Why is one kind of rhinoceros in more danger than the other one? *(They live in different habitats.)*

For more practice, go to MyELT.

PART 2 TEDTALKS

Photos from a storm chaser

CAMILLE SEAMAN'S idea worth spreading is that we should find ways to experience the natural forces that connect everything on the planet.

BEFORE YOU WATCH

A THINK CRITICALLY Predict. (page 32) 💡

Ask students to make connections to their own lives:

- Do you enjoy taking photos? If so, what do you take photos of? Why?
- When do you feel most connected to nature?

B (page 33)

C COMMUNICATE (page 33)

Ask students to look at the photo at the bottom of page 33 and describe how they would feel if they were standing where the men are.

VOCABULARY

D 🎧 1.17 (pages 34–35) Audio: 1:38 min

E COMMUNICATE (page 35)

For more practice, go to MyELT.

WATCH 🕐 Time: 40–50 min

F ▶ 1.6 WATCH FOR MAIN IDEAS (page 35)
Video: 3:30 min

WORDS IN THE TALK

Check understanding of *hail*, *lightning,* and *tactile*:

- What does *hail* look like?
- Is *lightning* dangerous? Explain.
- What are some *tactile* experiences you can have in nature?

> learn**more** (page 36) Ask students about their cultures: What group of people is native to your home country? Do those people still live there today? Do they still follow their original traditions?

NOTE-TAKING SKILL Use Abbreviations and Symbols (page 36)

Point out that students may already use abbreviations and symbols in texting and social media. Have students share any that may be helpful in the classroom. Emphasize that students should only use abbreviations and symbols in their notes that they will remember because they will often need to be able to read and understand their notes at a later date. Explain that they also have the option of going back to their notes after listening to fill in more details. Abbreviations and symbols are most useful *while* listening as a way to record as much information as possible in a short amount of time.

G ▶ 1.7 WATCH FOR DETAILS (page 36)
Video: 1:15 min

Have students come to the board and write specific symbols and abbreviations they may want to use before playing the video.

H COMMUNICATE (page 37) ☑

Have students write the information from their notes in full sentences and divide the sentences into thought groups before retelling the information to a partner.

I ▶ 1.8 WATCH FOR DETAILS (page 37)
Video: 1:18 min

J ▶ 1.9 EXPAND YOUR VOCABULARY (page 37) Video: 2:44 min

EXPANSION Check understanding of the vocabulary words by asking students to write their own sentences using each new term. Encourage them to use different forms of the verbs, for example:

- I tend to *stalk* my favorite celebrities online.
- *I was* laughing and *kidding* around with my friends before my teacher walked into the classroom.

For more practice, go to MyELT.

AFTER YOU WATCH 🕐 Time: 15–25 min

K THINK CRITICALLY Infer. (page 37) 💡

L COLLABORATE (page 38) ☑

Ask students to use both descriptive adectives and details to talk about the picture.

PUT IT TOGETHER ⏱ Time: 15–20 min

A THINK CRITICALLY Synthesize. (page 39) 💡

B THINK CRITICALLY Personalize. (page 39) 👥

21C SKILL Analyze Information. Ask students to work with a partner to make a chart that compares the danger, safety, and cost of each experience. Ask students to use their charts to further explain which experience they would prefer to have and why. Possible answers:

	PHOTO SAFARI	STORM CHASER
Danger	Close to wild animals	Close to storms
Safety	Led by a trained guide	Inside a van for protection
Cost	Expensive, but money donated to protect endangered animals	Just need a camera and a car

COMMUNICATE ◗ Time: 40–50 min + presentations

ASSIGNMENT **Give an Individual Presentation** about a time you felt a special connection to nature. (page 39)

ALTERNATE ASSIGNMENT Have students write a short story or present on a different topic.

- Have students use their outlines from exercise C (page 40) to write a short story using descriptive details and adjectives to describe a time they felt a special connection to nature. Then have students read their stories aloud to share their experiences.
- Alternative topics: A special connection to a family member (similar to Seaman's connection to her grandfather) or a special vacation when they felt connected to a new geographical area or group of people (similar to the photo safari).

PREPARE

PRESENTATION SKILL ▶ **1.10** Use Visual Aids (page 40) Video: 0:37 min

C–F (pages 40–41)

PRESENT

G–H THINK CRITICALLY Evaluate. (page 41)

REFLECT BOX (page 41) Have students work in small groups to review vocabulary use. Each student secretly chooses a word. Then the students take turns going around in a circle explaining their words. The group has to guess which word each student chose from the list. Have the students do the activity again, making sure not to choose words that were previously used.

For more practice, go to MyELT.

THINK AND DISCUSS (page 23)

1. Answers will vary. (E.g., feeling part of the natural world around you)   **2.** Answers will vary. (E.g., It shows people in a jeep that has cheetahs standing on top of it. They are connected to nature by being so close to these animals.)

PART 1

Photos from a Safari

A COMMUNICATE (page 24)

1. Answers will vary. (E.g., Africa, east Africa, Tanzania and Kenya)   **2.** Answers will vary. (E.g., A cheetah is chasing a wildebeest in Kenya.)   **3.** Answers will vary. (E.g., a trip to see animals in their natural habitat)

B THINK CRITICALLY Predict. (page 24)

1. a photo safari   **2.** as awesome
3. his reasons for going on a safari

C VOCABULARY (page 25)

1. cycle   **2.** essential   **3.** a couple of
4. motivation   **5.** chases   **6.** illegally
7. landscape   **8.** endangered   **9.** extinct
10. conservation

D COMMUNICATE (page 26)

Answers will vary.

E LISTEN FOR MAIN IDEAS (pages 26–27)

1. b, d   **2.** c, d, b, a

F LISTEN FOR DETAILS (page 27)

1. F; He spent 10 days.   **2.** T   **3.** F; Its landscape is flat.   **4.** T   **5.** F; A wildebeest is a member of the antelope family.   **6.** F; The lions were sleeping in the middle of the road. They never moved.   **7.** T   **8.** F; Tom accepted that that's how nature works.

G (page 28)

1. b   **2.** c   **3.** a   **4.** c   **5.** b

H THINK CRITICALLY Reflect. (page 28)

1. Answers will vary.   **2.** Answers will vary. (E.g., because it changes the ecosystem)
3. Answers will vary. (E.g., because people make money from animal parts; governments can fine people for selling or buying poached animal parts)   **4.** Answers will vary. (E.g., Everything in nature depends on something else, including humans.)

I (page 29)

Segment 1

1. a professional guide   **2.** they had seven seats   **3.** in tents, in a camp

Segment 2

4. female lions   **5.** in the middle of the road
6. lying, sleeping   **7.** about 10 feet away
8. for about 15 minutes

J COMMUNICATE (page 29)

Answers will vary.

K (pages 29–30)

1. The main point / was that countries like Kenya and Tanzania / rely on tourism / to pay for wildlife conservation. /   **2.** It covers / five thousand seven hundred / square miles. /
3. Here's a picture I took / at a drinking hole / early one morning. /   **4.** They're members of the antelope family. / They look kind of scary, / don't you think? /   **5.** One afternoon, / we were driving along, / and we saw these two female lions / lying in the middle of the road, / asleep. /
6. So our guide / stopped the jeep / about 10 feet away, / and we just sat there/ watching them / for about 15 minutes. /   **7.** Animals like gazelles / eat grass / and then animals like cheetahs / eat gazelles. /

L (page 30)

See answers for exercise K.

M (page 30)

Answers will vary. Suggested answers:

1.

A: Hey, Tom! / Welcome back! / How was your vacation? /

B: It was / . . . awesome. /

A: Oh, yeah? / Where did you go? /

B: I went to the Serengeti National Park. / I spent 10 days / on a photo safari. /

A: Wow! / What made you decide to do that? /

B: Well, / there were a couple of reasons. /

2.

A: It's so green. /

B: Yeah, / April is the rainy season. / It rained every day / on my trip. /

A: Did you travel alone, / or did you go with a guide? /

B: I went on a group tour / with a professional guide. / We traveled in jeeps / with seven seats, / and at night / we slept in tents / in a camp. /

N THINK CRITICALLY Interpret an Infographic. (pages 30–31)

1. to show how endangered the animals are **2.** decreasing; increasing **3.** 18
4. Critically Endangered **5.** Least Concern
6. Vulnerable **7.** Least Concern. Humans are included because we are part of nature, like other animals. **8.** Answers will vary.

PART 2 TEDTALKS

Photos from a storm chaser

A THINK CRITICALLY Predict. (page 32)

Answers will vary. (E.g., A *storm* is violent weather with a lot of wind, rain, thunder, lightning, or snow. A *storm chaser* is someone who follows storms for different reasons, such as curiosity, adventure, research, or media coverage. Seaman will probably talk about following storms to take pictures of them.)

B (page 33)

Answers will vary.

C COMMUNICATE (page 33)

Answers will vary.

D VOCABULARY (pages 34–35)

1. a **2.** b **3.** a **4.** c **5.** b **6.** a **7.** c
8. b **9.** b **10.** c

E COMMUNICATE (page 35)

Answers will vary.

F WATCH FOR MAIN IDEAS (page 35)

3.

G WATCH FOR DETAILS (page 36)

1. Everything = interconnected

2. Your water ⇒ cloud ⇒ rain

3. Super-cell clouds:

huge hail + spctclr tornadoes; 2% do

⇑ 50 m wide

⇑ 65,000 ft high

H COMMUNICATE (page 37)

Answers will vary.

I WATCH FOR DETAILS (page 37)

1. giant; super; grapefruit; spectacular
2. tactile; warm; charged; turquoise; straight

J EXPAND YOUR VOCABULARY (page 37)

1. b **2.** c **3.** a **4.** a

K THINK CRITICALLY Infer. (page 37)

1. Answers will vary. (E.g., "This" refers to the idea that "everything is interconnected." She means that her culture respects and understands their connection to nature.)
2. Answers will vary. (E.g., He used the example of how her sweat helps make a cloud that rains, and the rain helps the plants and animals. Another example from Part 1 is that animals like gazelles eat grass and then animals like cheetahs eat gazelles.) **3.** Because her daughter said she should **4.** Answers will vary. (E.g., She wants to express how powerful she thinks storms and lightning are.) **5.** Answers will vary. (E.g., because she thinks they are beautiful and dangerous) **6.** Answers will vary.

COLLABORATE (page 38)

Answers will vary.

PUT IT TOGETHER

A THINK CRITICALLY Synthesize. (page 39)

QUESTIONS	CONVERSATION: PHOTOS FROM A SAFARI	TED TALK: PHOTOS FROM A STORM CHASER
1. What was the setting? (place and time)	Serengeti National Park, recent vacation	Somewhere in the United States where there are tornadoes. Sometime after 2008.
2. What activity(ies) does the speaker describe?	Photo safari	Storm chasing
3. Why does the speaker do it?	He loves photography. Also, he wanted to help conservation efforts as a tourist.	Her daughter told her she should do it.
4. How does the speaker describe the experience?	He describes it as awesome. He uses many details to describe the landscape, the air, the tour, and the animals.	She describes it as tactile (physical) and exciting. She uses details to describe the clouds and the experience of storm chasing.
5. What makes the speaker feel connected to nature?	Seeing the cheetah kill the gazelle, he realized that everything in nature is connected. It's an endless cycle that people are part of.	Remembering her grandfather's lesson with the cloud. While storm chasing, she feels she is witnessing the forces that shaped everything in the universe.

B THINK CRITICALLY Personalize. (page 39)

Answers will vary.

C—REFLECT (pages 40–41)

Answers will vary.

PART 1

No Car, No Worries

Listening
Listen for Signposts

Note Taking
Indent Details

Speaking
Use Listing Signals

Pronunciation
Statement Intonation

PART 2

TEDTALKS

Sanjay Dastoor
A skateboard with a boost

PUT IT TOGETHER

Communicate
Participate in a Panel Discussion

Presentation Skill
Rehearse Your Presentation

UNIT THEME

By providing specific examples of eco-friendly transportation, Unit 3 explores the role of innovation in our efforts to reduce our carbon footprint.

ACADEMIC TRACK

Innovation

UNIT OPENER Time: 5–10 min

Ask guiding questions, such as:

- What does the caption say? *(Gigantic Sultan's Elephant—a moving sculpture in Nantes, France)*
- Which parts of the elephant look the most realistic? *(the tusks, the ears, the eye)*
- Would you like to ride on this elephant? Why, or why not?

THINK AND DISCUSS (page 43)

Possible answers:

1. *Traveling, moving, changing*
2. *People are riding on a mechanical elephant.*
3. *The photo shows a different way of getting around in Nantes, France.*

PART 1

No Car, No Worries ▶ **Slideshow available.**

The listening is a panel discussion about eco-friendly methods of transportation around the world. The three panel members discuss a cable car in Bolivia, ebikes in China, and electric microcars.

BEFORE YOU LISTEN Time: 30–40 min

A COMMUNICATE (page 44) 💡

Before doing the exercise, check understanding of *traffic*:

- What is *traffic?* *(cars and other vehicles moving on public roads or highways)*
- What time of day is traffic the heaviest? *(in the morning when people go to work, and in the evening when they go home)*
- Have you ever experienced really heavy traffic? How long were you in it? What did you do?

B 🎧**1.18** **COMMUNICATE** (page 44)
Audio: 0:48 min

VOCABULARY

C **⌒1.19** (page 45) Audio: 1:34 min

D **COMMUNICATE** (page 46)

For more practice, go to MyELT.

LISTEN ◑ Time: 40–50 min

> **LISTENING SKILL ⌒1.18** Listen for
> **Signposts** (page 46) Audio: 0:48 min
>
> Point out that signposts can be helpful tools
> for taking notes because they let you know
> when the speaker is moving on to a new topic.

E **⌒1.20 LISTEN FOR MAIN IDEAS** (page 47)
Audio: 0:45 min

> **NOTETAKING SKILL** Indent Details (page 47)
> Remind students that the note-taking format
> presented here is commonly used for outlines
> (see the Note-Taking Skill box on page 8),
> both when taking notes and when organizing
> or preparing a presentation. An outline
> provides a clear visual representation of how
> ideas or points are related to each other.
> Clarify use of indentation: main ideas are not
> indented, main details are indented once, and
> more specific details are indented twice, etc.

F **⌒1.21 ▶1.11 LISTEN FOR DETAILS**
(page 47) Audio: 2:09 min Video: 2:09 min 💡

Ask students to compare their notes to see if
they indented similar details (this can also be
used as a quick comprehension check before
hearing more of the panel discussion).

G **⌒1.22 ▶1.12 LISTEN FOR DETAILS**
(page 48) Audio: 1:22 min Video: 1:22 min

Remind students that being able to listen for
and note specific details, especially numbers,
can help them come to a deeper understanding
of the main concepts.

H **⌒1.23 ▶1.13** (page 48) Audio: 1:38 min
Video: 1:39 min

AFTER YOU LISTEN ◑ Time: 10–15 min

I **THINK CRITICALLY** Infer. (page 48) 💡

For more practice, go to MyELT.

SPEAKING ◑ Time: 45–55 min

> **SPEAKING SKILL** Use Listing Signals
> (page 48)
>
> Compare the listing signals to the signposts
> in the listening skill box on page 46. Remind
> students that they can use techniques they
> hear other speakers use to enhance their own
> speaking skills.

**For practice with the simple present tense,
go to MyELT.**

J **COMMUNICATE** (page 49)

Offer additional model language. (The next
advantage of the Tango car is...)

> **PRONUNCIATION SKILL ⌒1.24** Statement
> **Intonation** (page 50) Audio: 0:21 min

K **⌒1.25** (page 50) Audio: 0:53 min

L **⌒1.25** (page 50) Audio: 0:53 min

Encourage students to overemphasize the
intonation to get used to the rhythm of the
statements.

M **COLLABORATE** (page 50)

EXPANSION Ask students to divide their
sentences into thought groups before having
their partner read them with rising-falling
intonation. Refer them to the Pronunciation Skill
box on page 29 for a review of thought groups.

N **COMMUNICATE** (page 51)

Give students time to think about what
questions they will need to ask to get this
information. For example: Have you ridden a
cable car? Do you own a car?

For practice, go to MyELT.

PART 2 TEDTALKS

A skateboard with a boost

SANJAY DASTOOR'S idea worth spreading is that with a little creative thinking, you can turn an everyday object such as a skateboard into a quick and eco-friendly way to get around the city.

BEFORE YOU WATCH ◑ Time: 35–45 min

A THINK CRITICALLY Predict. (page 53)

Ask students how they get to work or school.

B COMMUNICATE (page 53)

C COMMUNICATE (page 53) 👥

Ask students to share any experience they have riding skateboards with the class.

21C SKILL **Analyze Alternative Points of View.** Have students consider how a younger person or older person would answer these questions. Why might they answer them differently?

VOCABULARY

D 🎧 **1.26** (pages 53–54) Audio: 1:26 min

E COMMUNICATE (page 54)

For more practice, go to MyELT.

WATCH ◑ Time: 30–40 min

F ▶ **1.14** **WATCH FOR MAIN IDEAS** (page 55) Video: 4:20 min ✅

Ask students which signpost the speaker will most likely use first. (*Today I'm going to show you . . .*)

WORDS IN THE TALK

Check students' understanding of *maneuverable*:

- In what kinds of situations is it important to have a *maneuverable* vehicle? *(when driving on narrow streets)*
- Besides cars, what other things do we maneuver? *(shopping carts, bicycles, wheel chairs, vacuum cleaners)*

G ▶ **1.15** **WATCH FOR DETAILS** (page 56)
Video: 1:05 min

H ▶ **1.16** **WATCH FOR DETAILS** (page 56)
Video: 1:08 min ✅ 💡

Have students predict which information in the box is at the same level of detail as *Motor* and what information should be indented further to the right because it's more specific.

I ▶ **1.17** **WATCH FOR DETAILS** (page 56)
Video: 1:01 min

Ask students to compare their answers and explain what statements or phrases they heard in the video that helped them choose their answer. If necessary, play the video a second time and ask students to write down the specific phrases they heard for each true or false statement.

J ▶ **1.18** **EXPAND YOUR VOCABULARY** (page 56) Video: 2:46 min

Check understanding of the vocabulary words:

- What do you use a *wall outlet* for?
- What *novel concepts* did you learn recently?
- What are some *handheld* objects you use?
- Do you know any other *compelling facts* about transportation?

For more practice, go to MyELT.

AFTER YOU WATCH ◐ Time: 20–30 min

K THINK CRITICALLY Reflect. (page 57) ✅ 👥

Encourage students to use the different listing signals in the speaking skill box on page 48 as they discuss their answers to the questions.

> **learnmore** (page 57) Ask students about their lives and environments. How big do you think is your environmental footprint? Why? How much carbon dioxide do you think your home country produces compared to other countries?

L THINK CRITICALLY Interpret an Infographic. (page 58) 💡

Check understanding of the infographic:

- What does the infographic show? *(the carbon footprint of different methods of transportation)*

- How does it show this information? *(by giving the grams of carbon dioxide per passenger per kilometer for each method)*

PUT IT TOGETHER ⏱ Time: 15–25 min

A THINK CRITICALLY Synthesize. (page 59)

B THINK CRITICALLY Reflect. (page 59)

COMMUNICATE ⏱ Time: 40–50 min + presentations

> **ASSIGNMENT** **Participate in a Panel Discussion** about three eco-friendly methods of transportation. (page 59)
>
> **ALTERNATE ASSIGNMENT** Have students work individually or present on a different topic.
>
> - For individual presentations, ask each student to choose a different resource to focus on. Remind students that individual presentations can include more personal connections, such as a story about or past experience with the benefits, and country- or culture-specific benefits.
> - Alternative topics: ecofriendly methods of building houses, farming, manufacturing, etc.

PREPARE

C COLLABORATE (page 60)

D (page 60)

> **PRESENTATION SKILL** **Rehearse Your Presentation** (page 60)

E COLLABORATE (page 61)

F (page 61)

PRESENT

G (page 61)

> **EXPANSION** Ask students to take notes during each panel discussion for additional practice with the skills presented earlier in the unit: listening for signposts and statement intonation, and taking notes by indenting details.

H THINK CRITICALLY Evaluate. (page 61)

> **REFLECT BOX** (page 61) Have students work in small groups to sort the words by part of speech.
> - *Nouns: acceleration, benefit, capacity, component, performance, perspective, portability, range, remote control, reverse, survey, system, vehicle*
> - *Adjectives: alternative, convenient, narrow, sustainable*
> - *Verbs: charge, interact*
> - *Adverbs: definitely*

For more practice, go to MyELT.

THINK AND DISCUSS (page 43)

1. Answers will vary. (E.g., traveling, moving, changing)   **2.** Answers will vary. (E.g., People are riding on a mechanical elephant.)   **3.** Answers will vary. (E.g., it shows a different way of getting around in Nantes, France—by mechanical elephant.)

PART 1

No Car, No Worries

A COMMUNICATE (page 44)

1. Answers will vary. (E.g., The photo shows a lot of traffic in a city. It was taken in Xiamen, China.)   **2.** Answers will vary. (E.g., traffic, long commutes, difficulty parking, accidents)   **3.** Answers will vary.

B COMMUNICATE (page 44)

Answers will vary. (E.g., The speaker says that cars are not very ecofriendly. Alternative methods of transportation are different ways to travel that are better for the environment. An example is riding a bike.)

C VOCABULARY (page 45)

1. narrow   **2.** definitely   **3.** range
4. survey   **5.** benefit   **6.** convenient
7. capacity   **8.** alternatives
9. system   **10.** charge

D COMMUNICATE (page 46)

Answers will vary.

E LISTEN FOR MAIN IDEAS (page 47)

1. Miguel: To begin / cable car (Mi Teleférico)   **2.** Jean: I'm going to present / ebike (electric bicycle)   **3.** Yulia: My topic today is / electric microcars

F LISTEN FOR DETAILS (page 47)

Problems w/ travel to/from El Alto & La Paz

  took a long time

  dangerous

  noise

  traffic

  pollution

Benefits of Mi Teleférico system

  convenient

  fast

  cheap

  eco-friendly

G LISTEN FOR DETAILS (page 48)

1. 20–30   **2.** 18   **3.** 1,000; 1,500   **4.** 15
5. a penny

H (page 48)

1. T   **2.** F; Some microcars have three wheels.   **3.** T   **4.** T   **5.** F; It's the world's narrowest car.

I THINK CRITICALLY Infer. (page 48)

1. Answers will vary. (E.g., Cable car: nice view, ability to talk to people, fun; Ebike: good exercise, helpful for people with disabilities; Microcar: cute, fun)   **2.** Answers will vary. (E.g., Cable car: fixed schedule, fixed route; Ebike and microcar: expensive, dangerous in traffic, transports only 1–2 people, easy to steal (ebike), dependent on charging stations)   **3.** Answers will vary.

J COMMUNICATE (page 49)

Answers will vary.

K (page 50)

1. The Tele**fé**rico / operates on elec**tri**city. /

2. The Tele**fé**rico / has the ca**pac**ity /

to carry six-**hun**dred passengers / a **day**. /

3. Most **e**bikes / can travel **twen**ty / or **thir**ty /

miles per **hour**. /

4. Ebikes are expensive to **buy**, / but they're

cheap to **op**erate. /

5. **M**icrocars / are the **sm**allest cars /

on the **road.** /

6. The **Tan**go car / has **seats** /

for only **two** people. /

L (page 50)

See answers for exercise K.

M COLLABORATE (page 50)

Answers will vary.

N COMMUNICATE (page 51)

Answers will vary.

PART 2 TEDTALKS

A skateboard with a boost

A THINK CRITICALLY Predict. (page 53)

Answers will vary. (E.g., about improving a skateboard to use for commuting)

B COMMUNICATE (page 53)

Answers will vary.

C COMMUNICATE (page 53)

Answers will vary.

D VOCABULARY (pages 53–54)

1. interact 2. perspective 3. portability
4. acceleration 5. vehicles 6. components
7. sustainable 8. performance 9. reverse
10. remote controls

E COMMUNICATE (page 54)

Answers will vary.

F WATCH FOR MAIN IDEAS (page 55)

1. c   2. b   3. d

4. e   5. a

G WATCH FOR DETAILS (page 56)

1. less   2. carry   3. 15   4. 1,000, dollar

H WATCH FOR DETAILS (page 56)

Components

  Motor

    20 mph uphill

  battery

    6 miles of range

  bought at a toy store

    from remote control airplanes

I WATCH FOR DETAILS (page 56)

1. F; It uses 20 times less energy than a car.
2. N 3. N 4. T 5. N

J EXPAND YOUR VOCABULARY (page 56)

1. a   2. b

3. a   4. b

K THINK CRITICALLY Reflect. (page 57)

1. Answers will vary. (E.g., San Francisco has a lot of hills. A boosted skateboard would help you get up the hills with a lot less effort.)
2. Answers will vary. (E.g., It might be hard to learn how to ride it. You could get hurt if you fall off.) 3. Answers will vary. (E.g., someone who already knows how to ride a regular skateboard; someone who doesn't know how to ride a regular skateboard) 4. Answers will vary. (E.g., making bigger ebikes with seats for more people)

L THINK CRITICALLY Interpret an Infographic. (page 58)

1. by grams of CO_2 per passenger per kilometer 2. Best: walking and cycling. Worst: flying 3. A train has many passengers on it, so each person's footprint is smaller. A scooter's footprint is bigger because it can only carry one or two people. 4. Answers will vary. (Cable cars: between full train and full mini-bus; ebikes: same place as regular bike; electric microcar:

above a full small car; boosted board: same place as walking or cycling)

PUT IT TOGETHER

A **THINK CRITICALLY** Synthesize. (page 59)

Answers will vary. Possible answers:

Skateboard

range of 6 miles/10 km; speed of 20 mph/30kph; cheap to build; $1 to charge; light weight; small/easy to carry; charges in 15 minutes; no need for parking space

Ebike

range of 18 miles; speed of 20–30 mph; expensive to buy; $0.15 to charge; can get exercise; good for people who can't walk a lot; easy to park

Microcar

range of 100 miles; expensive to buy; easy to park; room for two passengers

All

go up hills; electric; cheap to charge; sustainable

B **THINK CRITICALLY** Reflect. (page 59)

Answers will vary.

C **COLLABORATE** (page 60)

Answers will vary.

D—REFLECT (pages 60–61)

Answers will vary.

PART 1

What's Your Music-Listening Style?

Listening
Listen for Reasons

Speaking
Give Reasons

Pronunciation
Contractions with *Be*

PART 2

TEDTALKS

Daria van den Bercken
Why I take the piano on the road . . . and in the air

Note Taking
Write Key Words or Short Sentences

PUT IT TOGETHER

Communicate
Give an Individual Presentation

Presentation Skill
Use an Effective Hook

UNIT THEME

Unit 4 explores the importance of music in our lives and highlights how people listen to music differently.

ACADEMIC TRACK

Music

UNIT OPENER Time: 5–10 min

Ask guiding questions, such as:

- Where was this picture taken? *(outside, possibly in someone's yard, in Arkansas)*
- How old is the girl? *(young, a child, 6 or 7 years old)*

THINK AND DISCUSS (page 63)

Possible answers:

1. *Yes. It can be played or heard in many different places.*
2. *The girl is sitting in the back of a truck and playing a piano. Maybe the piano is in the back of the truck because someone is moving it.*

PART 1

What's Your Music-Listening Style?

The listening is a radio talk show. The host interviews four people on the street about what type of music they listen to the most and what they do while they're listening to music.

BEFORE YOU LISTEN Time: 30–40 min

A COMMUNICATE (page 64)

Ask students questions about the picture to check their comprehension of key concepts:

- Who are the people? *(musicians)*
- What instruments are they holding? *(from left: saxophone, clarinet, drum, sousaphone)*
- What kind of music do they play? *(marching band music)*
- Why do they play their music? *(for entertainment, competition)*

B COLLABORATE (page 64)

Encourage students to include their own favorite types of music. If there is a type of music on a list that is not familiar to all students, encourage the students who listed it to explain it to the rest of the class.

VOCABULARY

C 🎧 **1.27** (pages 65–66) Audio: 2:02 min

D COMMUNICATE (page 66)

For more practice, go to MyELT.

LISTEN ◑ Time: 30–40 min

E 🎧 **1.28** **LISTEN FOR MAIN IDEAS** (page 67)
Audio: 3:27 min

F 🎧 **1.29** **LISTEN FOR DETAILS** (page 67)
Audio: 1:10 min

G 🎧 **1.30** **LISTEN FOR DETAILS** (page 67)
Audio: 1:09 min

Ask students to make connections between the genres of music in exercise E and the listening styles in exercise G. Ask guiding questions such as: What type of music do you like to listen to while you are driving? Working? Doing your homework? Do you ever sit and listen to music without doing anything else? If so, what kind of music do you listen to then?

LISTENING SKILL Listen for Reasons (page 67)

H 🎧 **1.31** (page 68) Audio: 1:31 min

Have students go over their answers with a partner in statement form using *because* and *so* to give reasons for each speaker's choice of music. For example: *Speaker 4 likes jazz because it is relaxing. Speaker 2 needs to focus at work, so she listens to rock music.* Then, ecourage students to use *because* and *so* to tell their partners reasons why they like certain types of music.

AFTER YOU LISTEN ◑ Time: 25–35 min

I THINK CRITICALLY Analyze. (page 68)

J (page 68)

K (page 69)
Ensure that students know all the music genres listed in the quiz. If possible, play brief clips of the different genres.

L (page 70)
If possible, group students by the personality types they received on the quiz.

For more practice, go to MyELT.

SPEAKING ◑ Time: 25–35 min

SPEAKING SKILL Give Reasons (page 70)

M THINK CRITICALLY Personalize. (page 70)

PRONUNCIATION SKILL 🎧 **1.32** Contractions with *Be* (page 71) Audio: 0:35 min

Ask students if they know of or have heard any other contractions with *be*. For example: *there's, that's.* Go over the different pronunciation of the final -*s* in the contractions. The final -*s* in *what's*, *it's*, and *that's* makes an "s" sound. The final -*s* in *she's*, *who's*, *he's*, and *there's* makes a "z" sound.

For practice with contractions with *be*, go to MyELT.

N 🎧 **1.33** (page 71) Audio: 0:35 min

O (page 71)

For more practice, go to MyELT.

PART 2 TEDTALKS

Why I take the piano on the road . . . and in the air

DARIA VAN DEN BERCKEN'S idea worth spreading is that we should try to enjoy music the way a child does—full of wonder and with pure amazement.

BEFORE YOU WATCH ◑ Time: 35–45 min

A THINK CRITICALLY Predict. (page 72)
Ask students to make connections to their own experience with music:

- Have you been to a concert or musical performance in a unique setting before? What was it like? How did it make you feel?

B COMMUNICATE (page 73)

VOCABULARY

C 🎧 **1.34** (pages 73–74) Audio: 2:13 min

D COMMUNICATE (page 74)

For more practice, go to MyELT.

WATCH ⏱ Time: 45–55 min

> learn**more** (page 75) Ask students: Who are some other famous composers? What types of music did they create? What are the titles of some of their famous pieces of music?

E ▶**1.19** **WATCH FOR MAIN IDEAS** (page 75)
Video: 9:36 min

WORDS IN THE TALK

Check understanding of *browsing, melancholic,* and *the media*:

- When do you *browse* the Internet? Is it helpful? Why, or why not?
- What are some *melancholic* songs or movies that you know?
- What are some ways that *the media* influences your life?

F THINK CRITICALLY Reflect. (page 75)

> **NOTE-TAKING SKILL** **Write Key Words or Short Sentences** (page 75)
>
> Tell students that writing key words and short sentences is a slightly more detailed way of taking notes than the one they learned in the Note-Taking Skill box on page 26 (abbreviations and symbols), and that this note-taking method can be used in combination with the indenting details skill learned in the Note-Taking Skill box on page 47.

G ▶**1.20** **WATCH FOR DETAILS** (page 76)
Video: 9:45 min 💡

H CHECK YOUR NOTES (page 76)

I ▶**1.21** **WATCH FOR REASONS** (page 76)
Video: 0:40 min ✅

Ask students which word helped them identify her reason. Did it introduce or follow the reason? *(The word* because *introduced the reason.)*

J ▶**1.22** **EXPAND YOUR VOCABULARY**
(page 77) Video: 2:38 min

EXPANSION Ask students to interview each other by writing and asking questions that use the phrases from the TED Talk. For example: *What are some things that are part of your* day-to-day *life? Are* you *in awe of* anything? Encourage students to ask for reasons based on their partner's answers. For example:

A: Are *you* in awe of *anything?*
B: Yes, *I'm* in awe of *how well some people play music.*
A: *Why does that amaze you so much?*
B: *The reason that it amazes me is I'm not very good at playing music.*

For more practice, go to MyELT.

AFTER YOU WATCH ⏱ Time: 15–25 min

K COMMUNICATE (page 77) 👥

L THINK CRITICALLY Interpret an Infographic. (page 78) 💡

Check understanding of the infographic:

- What does the infographic show? *(how much time each week people spend listening to music in different situations)*
- How many different situations are shown? *(five)*
- Which situation includes more than one activity? *(Listening while doing other activities alone)*
- How does it compare the information? *(by giving percentages of total listening time; by using a bar graph)*

M COMMUNICATE (page 78)

PUT IT TOGETHER ⏱ Time: 15–25 min

A THINK CRITICALLY Synthesize. (page 79) 💡

B (page 79)

COMMUNICATE ⏱ Time: 40–50 min + presentations

> **ASSIGNMENT** **Give an Individual Presentation** about your music listening style. (page 79)
>
> **ALTERNATE ASSIGNMENT** Have students interview each other about their music preferences and listening styles, or have them present on a different topic.
>
> - For an interview, one student (the interviewer) should write out specific questions to ask 2–3 classmates (interviewees). The interviewees should prepare to answer the questions by thinking about their own music preferences and listening styles.
> - An alternative topic is to have students who play music share their experiences playing music in front of other people.

PREPARE

> **PRESENTATION SKILL** ▶ **1.23** **Use an Effective Hook** (page 80) Video: 0:24 min
>
> Remind students that a hook can be used as a way to get an audience's attention by making a connection to a famous person, a personal experience, or to information they did not already know. By making a connection with the audience, students can give more effective and interesting presentations.

C (page 80)

D COLLABORATE (page 81)

E (page 81)

PRESENT

F (page 81)

G THINK CRITICALLY Evaluate. (page 81)

> **REFLECT BOX** (page 81) Have students play the game "Taboo" to review definitions and synonyms. Students get in pairs. Partner A sits facing the whiteboard, and Partner B sits with back to the whiteboard. To begin the game, write one of the vocabulary words in big letters on the whiteboard. Be sure that all students facing the whiteboard can read the word. Students must remain silent and still until you say, "Go!" When you say, "Go!" Partner A has one minute to get Partner B to say the word or phrase written on the board. Partner A may only use verbal clues and cannot say any part of the vocabulary term. After one minute, students switch seats and roles, and the game repeats.

For more practice, go to MyELT.

THINK AND DISCUSS (page 63)

1. Answers will vary. (E.g., Yes. It can be played or heard in many different places.)   **2.** Answers will vary. (E.g., The girl is sitting in the back of a truck playing a piano. Maybe the piano is in the back of the truck because someone is moving it.)

PART 1

What's Your Music-Listening Style?

A COMMUNICATE (page 64)

Answers will vary.

B COLLABORATE (page 64)

Answers will vary. (E.g., rock, blues, folk, soundtracks, dance, electronic, soul, R&B, house, reggae, bluegrass, country, funk, heavy metal, jazz, oldies, opera, pop)

C VOCABULARY (pages 65–66)

1. a   **2.** b   **3.** c   **4.** b   **5.** a   **6.** a   **7.** c
8. a   **9.** c   **10.** a

D COMMUNICATE (page 66)

Answers will vary.

E LISTEN FOR MAIN IDEAS (page 67)

Speaker 1: classical

Speaker 2: rock

Speaker 3: roots music

Speaker 4: jazz

F LISTEN FOR DETAILS (page 67)

1. study; 25   **2.** listen; do   **3.** street

G LISTEN FOR DETAILS (page 67)

1. c   **2.** d   **3.** a   **4.** b

H (page 68)

Speaker 1: d

Speaker 2: b

Speaker 3: c

Speaker 4: a

I THINK CRITICALLY Analyze. (page 68)

Answers will vary.

J (page 68)

Answers will vary.

K (page 69)

Answers will vary.

L (page 70)

Answers will vary.

M THINK CRITICALLY Personalize. (page 70)

Answers will vary.

N (page 71)

1. a   **2.** a   **3.** b   **4.** a   **5.** b   **6.** b

O (page 71)

1. Today <u>we're</u> talking about music.

2. <u>There's</u> music all around us.

3. <u>That's</u> a lot of listening.

4. Do they do other things while <u>they're</u> listening?

5. <u>It's</u> a big category.

6. <u>What's</u> your music listening style?

PART 2 TEDTALKS

Why I take the piano on the road . . . and in the air

A THINK CRITICALLY Predict. (page 72)

Answers will vary. (E.g., why she loves classical music; why she plays music in unusual places)

B COMMUNICATE (page 73)

Answers will vary.

C VOCABULARY (pages 73–74)

1. constant   **2.** elements   **3.** composer
4. energetic   **5.** relate to   **6.** magical
7. reach   **8.** prejudice   **9.** contrasting
10. complexity

D COMMUNICATE (page 74)

Answers will vary.

E WATCH FOR MAIN IDEAS (page 75)

1., 3.

F THINK CRITICALLY Reflect. (page 75)

Answers will vary.

G WATCH FOR DETAILS (page 76)

Segment 1

1. Answers will vary. (E.g., played Handel flying: Brazil)

2. Answers will vary. (E.g., played Handel while driving: Amsterdam)

3. Answers will vary. (E.g., amazed by Handel keyboard music because of its sound)

4. Answers will vary. (E.g., found it on Internet)

5. Answers will vary. (E.g., Handel piece sad, then energetic)

Segment 2

1. Answers will vary. (E.g., children 7–8: open, willing, comfortable listening to music; listen without prejudice)

2. Answers will vary. (E.g., children 11–12: complexity an issue; others' opinions count; prejudiced)

H CHECK YOUR NOTES (page 76)

Answers will vary.

I WATCH FOR REASONS (page 76)

Answers will vary. (E.g., She fell in love with the music, and she wanted to share it with everyone.)

J EXPAND YOUR VOCABULARY (page 77)

1. a **2.** b **3.** b **4.** a

K COMMUNICATE (page 77)

1. Answers will vary. (E.g., tell them about it; invite them to try it with you) **2.** Answers will vary.

L THINK CRITICALLY Interpret an Infographic. (page 78)

1. False; 23 percent **2.** False; in the car
3. True **4.** True **5.** False; 13 percent

M COMMUNICATE (page 78)

Answers will vary.

PUT IT TOGETHER

A THINK CRITICALLY Synthesize. (page 79)

Someone in the Interview: a, d

Both: b, e, g, i

van den Bercken: c, f, h

B (page 79)

Answers will vary.

C—REFLECT (pages 80–81)

Answers will vary.

PART 1

The Power of Gratitude

Listening
Listen for Key Words and Phrases

Note Taking
Use a Mind Map

Speaking
Support Ideas with Examples

Pronunciation
Sentence Stress

PART 2

TEDTALKS

Jarrett J. Krosoczka
Why lunch ladies are heroes

PUT IT TOGETHER

Communicate
Give an Individual Presentation

Presentation Skill
Tell a Personal Story

UNIT THEME

Unit 5 explores the benefits and

effects of gratitude in our lives.

ACADEMIC TRACK

Sociology

UNIT OPENER   Time: 5–10 min

Ask guiding questions, such as:

- What is the woman in the picture doing? *(She is covering her mouth because she is surprised and happy.)*
- What are the students in the picture doing? *(They are clapping for the woman.)*

THINK AND DISCUSS (page 83)

Possible answers:

1. *The title means that we should be thankful for the things we have, and express thanks to those who have helped us in some way.*

2. *Sakhalin Finnie looks very surprised, happy, and excited. The people in the audience look happy and excited for Finnie, too. She probably received the award because she is a good teacher and students enjoy learning with her.*

PART 1

The Power of Gratitude ▶ **Slideshow available.**

The listening is a professional presentation about the benefits of gratitude for people who give and receive it.

BEFORE YOU LISTEN   Time: 30–40 min

A COMMUNICATE (page 84)

Ask the students how they say *thank you* in their languages, and whether there is more than one way to say *thank you*. *(In English, people say* thank you *and* thanks.*)*

B THINK CRITICALLY Predict. (page 84)

VOCABULARY

C   2.2 (page 85) Audio: 1:29 min

D COMMUNICATE (page 86)

For more practice, go to MyELT.

LISTEN ⏱ Time: 30–40 min

E 🎧 **2.3** ▶ **1.24** **LISTEN FOR MAIN IDEAS**
(page 86) Audio: 4:14 min Video: 4:11 min

> **LISTENING SKILL** 🎧 **2.4** **Listen for Key Words and Phrases** (page 86) Audio: 0:18 min
>
> Have students complete a two-column synonym chart for the vocabulary words on page 85. The first column should contain the vocabulary words, and in the second column, the students should list synonyms for the words. They can include information from the definitions, but should also add their own ideas or look up other synonyms in a dictionary.

F 🎧 **2.3** (page 87) Audio: 4:14 min

> **NOTE-TAKING SKILL** **Use a Mind Map** (page 87)
>
> Remind students that this skill is similar to the Note-Taking Skill they learned on page 47 (Indent Details), but shows the relationships between ideas in a different way. The details are still grouped around the main idea they support, but they are organized with bubbles and lines instead of indentation.

G 🎧 **2.5** **LISTEN FOR DETAILS** (page 87)

Audio: 1:56 min

Ask students about the relationships among the ideas:

- Why does the *Grateful people* bubble appear above the other two, and have a line connecting it to both? *(It's the main idea.)*
- What goes in the green bubbles under the *Physical benefits* and *Mental benefits* bubbles? *(specific details about those benefits)*

H 🎧 **2.6** **LISTEN FOR DETAILS** (page 88)

Audio: 1:32 min

I 🎧 **2.7** **LISTEN FOR DETAILS** (page 88)

Audio: 1:09 min

Have students work in pairs to write two more tips for becoming more grateful with the two extra words. They may change the form of the words if they need to. *(Every day,* write down things that happened that you are grateful for. If

you are pleased with something that someone has done, tell them.)

AFTER YOU LISTEN ⏱ Time: 15–25 min

J **THINK CRITICALLY** Analyze. (page 88) 💡

K **THINK CRITICALLY** Personalize. (page 89)

L **COMMUNICATE** (page 89)

> **21C SKILL** **Evaluate Beliefs.** Have students rank the statements in order of importance for them. 1 is the most important and 8 is the least important. Then have them compare their rankings with a partner.

For more practice, go to MyELT.

SPEAKING ⏱ Time: 30–40 min

> **SPEAKING SKILL** **Support Ideas with Examples** (page 90)
>
> Tell students that examples can enhance a presentation because they help make ideas more relevant to the audience's personal experiences.

M 🎧 **2.8** **COLLABORATE** (page 90) Audio: 1:02 min

Remind students that *gratitude* is the abstract concept the speaker is trying to explain through multiple examples. Ask them which examples best help them understand this concept.

N **COMMUNICATE** (page 91) 💡

> **PRONUNCIATION SKILL** 🎧 **2.9** **Sentence Stress** (page 91) Audio: 0:16 min
>
> **EXPANSION** Have students practice stressing different words in the two example sentences. Ask them how it changes the focus of what the most important information is. For example:
>
> - Today, **we're** going to be discussing gratitude. *(Emphasizing* we're *indicates that the people in the audience are important participants in the discussion.)*
> - Today, we're going to be **discussing** gratitude. *(Emphasizing* discussing *focuses on the fact that the participants will be talking about gratitude, not reading or writing about it.)*

O 🎧 **2.10** (page 91) Audio: 0:48 min

Ask students why they think the speaker chose to emphasize the words in each sentence. *(In items 3 and 4, physical and mental are emphasized because the speaker wants to make it clear that she is talking about two different areas of health.)*

P 🎧 **2.10** (page 91) Audio: 0:48 min

Have students experiment with stressing different words in the sentences to further understand how altering the stress can alter the focus.

Q COMMUNICATE (page 91)

For more practice, go to MyELT.

PART 2 TEDTALKS

Why lunch ladies are heroes

JARRETT J. KROSOCZKA'S idea worth spreading is that a simple "thank you" can change the life of the giver and the receiver.

BEFORE YOU WATCH ⏱ Time: 35–45 min

A THINK CRITICALLY Predict. (page 92)

Ask students about the quote:

- How can a *thank you* change a life? Use examples from the presentation in Part 1 and your own ideas. *(by making the person who says or receives it happier and healthier; by opening new opportunities for people)*

B (page 93)

C COMMUNICATE (page 93) ☑

Have students underline which words they think should be stressed in B, and stress those words when they ask their partner the questions.

> learn**more** (page 93) Ask students about their experience: Did you ever express gratitude to the people who worked in the cafeteria or did other jobs at your school?

VOCABULARY

D 🎧 **2.11** (pages 94–95) Audio: 1:53 min

E COMMUNICATE (page 95)

For more practice, go to MyELT.

WATCH ⏱ Time: 30–40 min

F ▶ **1.25 WATCH FOR MAIN IDEAS** (page 95)

Video: 5:25 min

WORDS IN THE TALK

Check understanding of *guidance counselor:*

- What are some reasons a student might see a *guidance counselor? (to discuss problems at school, to get advice about what classes to take)*

G THINK CRITICALLY Reflect. (page 95)

Offer any relevant experiences from your own time at school as examples of other school heroes. *(teachers who spent time helping their students outside of class; librarians who were always available to help you find books)*

H ▶ **1.26 WATCH FOR DETAILS** (pages 96–97)

Video: 5:40 min

I ▶ **1.27 GIVE EXAMPLES** (page 97)

Video: 1:22 min ☑

Ask students how the things kids did and the things lunch ladies did were connected. *(They were part of School Lunch Hero Day. Kids made comics and vases to celebrate the things their lunch ladies did for them all year.)*

J ▶ **1.28 EXPAND YOUR VOCABULARY**

(page 97) Video: 2:28 min

EXPANSION Ask students to use each vocabulary word to describe an example of gratitude from their own lives.

For more practice, go to MyELT.

AFTER YOU WATCH ⏱ Time: 15–25 min

K THINK CRITICALLY Analyze. (page 97) 💡

EXPANSION Have students work in small groups to write a letter thanking someone at their school who helps them. They should use specific examples of things the person has done. After, the students can give the letter to the person they wrote it to.

L THINK CRITICALLY Interpret an Infographic. (page 98) 💡

Check understanding of *charity* and *psychology*:

- *Charity* means helping others by giving time or money. What are some ways to be involved with charity? *(volunteer, donate money or clothes to the poor)*
- *Psychology* is the study of human behavior. What professions use information learned from psychology? *(therapy, marketing, politics)*

PUT IT TOGETHER 🕐 Time: 15–20 min

A THINK CRITICALLY Synthesize. (page 99) 💡

Alternately, students could rewrite the chart as three mind maps: the questions are the main bubbles and the information from the presentation and the TED Talk is placed in two bubbles connected to the main one.

B THINK CRITICALLY Personalize. (page 99) 👥

COMMUNICATE 🕐 Time: 40–50 min + presentations

> **ASSIGNMENT** Give an Individual **Presentation** about a time when giving or receiving gratitude affected you or someone you know. (page 99)
>
> **ALTERNATE ASSIGNMENT** Alternate topic: a time when you did not express gratitude for something someone else did for you. The students can still use the personal story notes on page 100.

PREPARE

> **PRESENTATION SKILL** Tell a Personal Story (page 100)
>
> Remind students that personal stories can be effective examples to help explain a concept or support an idea. Ask students to share any stories they have heard that helped them understand something better.

For practice with the simple past, go to MyELT.

C (page 100)

D COLLABORATE (page 100)

As one student practices his or her presentation, the other listens and notes the key words and phrases used.

E (page 100)

PRESENT

F (page 101)

Have students take notes on one presentation using a mind map. The name of the presenter goes in the main bubble. Six bubbles go around the one with the presenter's name and should include the following information about the event: when, where, who, what happened, the ending, what was learned. Collect these to check students' use of mind maps.

G THINK CRITICALLY Evaluate. (page 101)

> **REFLECT BOX** (page 101) Have students choose one of the class presentations, other than their own, and retell it in pairs. Ask them to include as many of the unit's vocabulary words in their summary as possible. As the speaker retells the idea, the listener puts a check next to each word used. The speaker gets a check for every time he or she uses a word. At the end of the summary, the listener counts the total number of checks. The partner that has the most checks wins.

For more practice, go to MyELT.

THINK AND DISCUSS (page 83)

1. Answers will vary. (E.g., The title means that we should be thankful for the things we have, and express thanks to those who have helped us in some way.)   2. Answers will vary. (E.g., Sakhalin Finnie looks very surprised, happy, and excited. The people in the audience look happy and excited for Finnie, too. She probably received the award because she is a good teacher that students enjoy learning with.)

PART 1

The Power of Gratitude

A COMMUNICATE (page 84)

Answers will vary.

B THINK CRITICALLY Predict. (page 84)

Answers will vary.

C VOCABULARY (page 85)

1. affect   2. aware of   3. acknowledges
4. expresses   5. grateful   6. recognizing
7. productive   8. attitude   9. stress
10. researchers

D COMMUNICATE (page 86)

Answers will vary.

E LISTEN FOR MAIN IDEAS (page 86)

b

F (page 87)

All items should be checked at least once. The speaker uses *gratitude* the most.

G LISTEN FOR DETAILS (page 87)

Physical benefits: a, d, e
Mental benefits: b, c, f

H LISTEN FOR DETAILS (page 88)

1. b   2. c   3. a

I LISTEN FOR DETAILS (page 88)

1. write down   2. thank you   3. notice
4. actions

J THINK CRITICALLY Analyze. (page 88)

1. Answers will vary. (E.g., Yes, the presenter believes that we can all become grateful people. She gave us specific steps to follow if we want to be more grateful.)   2. Answers will vary.

K THINK CRITICALLY Personalize. (page 89)

Answers will vary.

L COMMUNICATE (page 89)

Answers will vary.

M COLLABORATE (page 90)

1. the meaning of gratitude: a feeling of thankfulness; a feeling of appreciation; being aware of the good things in life; appreciating small things; counting your blessings   2. how gratitude affects people who receive it: it can make them more helpful; The people he thanked gave more help.

N COMMUNICATE (page 91)

1. Any three of the following: a feeling of thankfulness; a feeling of appreciation; being aware of the good things in life; appreciating small things; counting your blessings   2. by referring to a study that shows they are more helpful

O (page 91)

1. So, what do you think I mean by gratitude?   2. It's a feeling of thankfulness, a feeling of appreciation.   3. They're finding that grateful people have better physical health.
4. Grateful people have better mental health, too.   5. Gratitude is important at work as well.   6. Gratitude can affect the person who receives thanks, too.

P (page 91)

See answers for exercise O.

Q COMMUNICATE (page 91)

1. Answers will vary. (E.g., stressed words: Who is the happiest person you know? Why do you think he or she is happy?)   2. Answers will vary. (E.g., stressed words: Are you a productive person? What are some ways to

be more productive?)   **3.** Answers will vary.
(E.g., stressed words: What are some ways to
acknowledge someone who helps you, such as
a teacher?)

PART 2 TEDTALKS

Why lunch ladies are heroes

A THINK CRITICALLY Predict. (page 92)

Answers will vary.

B (page 93)

Answers will vary.

C COMMUNICATE (page 93)

Answers will vary.

D VOCABULARY (pages 94–95)

1. participate   **2.** imagination   **3.** response
4. programs   **5.** create   **6.** attended
7. treated   **8.** inspired   **9.** encounter
10. rely on

E COMMUNICATE (page 95)

Answers will vary.

F WATCH FOR MAIN IDEAS (page 95)

1., 2., 4., 5.

G THINK CRITICALLY Reflect. (page 95)

Answers will vary.

H WATCH FOR DETAILS (pages 96–97)

Segment 1

1. school   **2.** idea   **3.** fish   **4.** monsters
5. served

Segment 2

1. kids   **2.** lunch ladies   **3.** recognize

Segment 3

1. serve   **2.** problems   **3.** food

Segment 4

1. important   **2.** changes   **3.** expresses

I GIVE EXAMPLES (page 97)

Things kids did: a, d

Things lunch ladies did: b, c

J EXPAND YOUR VOCABULARY (page 97)

1. a   **2.** b   **3.** a   **4.** b

K THINK CRITICALLY Analyze. (page 97)

1. Answers will vary. (E.g., He compares lunch
ladies with superheroes who fight crime with fish
stick nunchucks. The audience laughs because
lunch ladies aren't usually seen this way.)
2. Answers will vary. (E.g., Lunch ladies are
often not appreciated for their work. Students
don't always talk to them, and they are often
ignored.)

L THINK CRITICALLY Interpret an Infographic.
(page 98)

1. benefits   **2.** 20 percent   **3.** 10 percent
4. 7 percent   **5.** South Africa, Denmark
6. feelings, 7 years

PUT IT TOGETHER

A THINK CRITICALLY Synthesize. (page 99)

QUESTIONS	PRESENTATION: THE POWER OF GRATITUDE	TED TALK: WHY LUNCH LADIES ARE HEROES
1. What are some ways to show gratitude?	• say thank you more often • thank people around you who do kind things	• _say thank you_ to lunch ladies • children became very creative: they made gifts for their lunch ladies
2. How does gratitude affect people who give thanks?	• have better physical health • have better mental health	• According to Krosoczka, gratitude changes the life of the person who expresses it.
3. How does gratitude affect people who receive thanks?	• In a study, people became more helpful when a student thanked them. • It feels good to help. • When you feel good, you want to be even more helpful.	• School Lunch Hero Day made one lunch lady feel important.

B THINK CRITICALLY Personalize. (page 99)

Answers will vary.

C—REFLECT (pages 100–101)

Answers will vary.

UNIT 6   Tell Me Why . . .

UNIT THEME

Unit 6 explores the importance of asking questions, experimenting, and exploring the things we are each curious about as an integral part of the learning process.

ACADEMIC TRACK

Education

UNIT OPENER Time: 5–10 min

Ask guiding questions, such as:

- What is the machine in the picture doing? *(giving off electricity)*
- Where was this picture taken? *(in a man's yard)*
- Would you try something like this in your yard? Why, or why not?

THINK AND DISCUSS (page 103)

Possible answers:

1. *The title suggests that we ask "why" when we are curious about something. Children and researchers usually ask this question.*

2. *Terren might make his sculptures because he's interested in the way electricity looks.*

PART 1

Benefits of Curiosity ▶ **Slideshow available.**

The listening is a conversation between three students about the importance of being curious. They discuss their own curiosity and what researchers are uncovering about curiosity: the brain responds to curiosity the same way that it responds to a reward, and people remember information better when they are curious.

BEFORE YOU LISTEN ⏱ Time: 30–40 min

A COMMUNICATE (page 104) 💡

Before students start the exercise, have them cover the caption and try to guess what it says.

B   2.12 THINK CRITICALLY Predict.
(page 104) Audio: 0:34 min 💡

Encourage students to think about their own answers to Juan's question. Remind them to give examples to support their answers, as they learned in the Speaking Skill box on page 90.

VOCABULARY

C 🎧 **2.13** (page 105) Audio: 1:44 min

D **COMMUNICATE** (page 106)

For more practice, go to MyELT.

LISTEN 🕐 Time: 35–45 min

E 🎧 **2.14 LISTEN FOR MAIN IDEAS**
(page 106) Audio: 3:57 min

Ask students if they can remember the two
main findings of the research study. (*It feels
good to be curious, and when we're curious, we
remember information more easily.*)

> learn**more** (page 106) Ask students:
> How are students expected to participate
> in class in your countries? Is it common
> to ask a lot of questions? In what ways
> can you demonstrate how much you know
> about the content, as well as your individual
> perspective in a class?

F 🎧 **2.15 LISTEN FOR DETAILS** (page 107)
Audio: 2:26 min

Have students individually check the
descriptions in item 1 that are true for them, and
then compare their answers with a partner.

G 🎧 **2.16 LISTEN FOR DETAILS** (page 107)
Audio: 1:45 min

LISTENING SKILL 🎧 **2.17** **Make Inferences**
(page 108) Audio: 0:20 min

H 🎧 **2.18 MAKING INFERENCES** (page 108)
Audio: 2:04 min

Ask students to explain how they made these
inferences: Was it what the speaker said, or how
he or she said it?

AFTER YOU LISTEN 🕐 Time: 10–15 min

I **THINK CRITICALLY** Reflect. (page 109) 💬
Explain that "curiosity killed the cat" means that
being too interested in finding out information

can get you in trouble. Ask students to share
similar expressions in their languages.

For more practice, go to MyELT.

SPEAKING 🕐 Time: 45–55 min

SPEAKING SKILL **Show Interest** (page 109)

**For practice with *Yes/No* and *Wh-* questions,
go to MyELT.**

J 🎧 **2.19** (page 109) Audio: 1:37 min

K **COMMUNICATE** (page 109) 💡

L **COMMUNICATE** (page 110)

PRONUNCIATION SKILL 🎧 **2.20** **Intonation in
Questions** (page 110) Audio: 0:26 min

Ask students to repeat the two questions
to practice mimicking the rising and falling
intonation.

M 🎧 **2.21** (page 110) Audio: 0:37 min

N **COMMUNICATE** (page 110)
EXPANSION Have students use these questions
to conduct a survey of people outside the class.
Each student should survey five people. When
they share their results with the class, they
should also explain any inferences they made
about what the speakers said, or how they said
it. For example, could they infer if the speakers
think being a curious person is good or bad?

O **THINK CRITICALLY** Interpret an Infographic.
(page 111) 💬

Check understanding of the infographic:

• What does the infographic show? (*a
  comparison of what subjects are most written
  about on Wikipedia, and the education level of
  Wikipedia users*)

• How is the information shown? (*through
  graphs and percentages*)

For more practice, go to MyELT.

PART 2 TEDTALKS

3 rules to spark learning

RAMSEY MUSALLAM'S idea worth spreading is that curiosity provides powerful motivation for learning new things, both inside and outside the classroom.

BEFORE YOU WATCH ⏱ Time: 35–45 min

A (page 112) 👥

Read the quote together and ask students what it means. *(Students need to be curious before they can learn. Curiosity is the most important thing in education.)*

B COMMUNICATE (pages 112–113) 👥

VOCABULARY

C 🎧 **2.22** (pages 113–114) Audio: 1:35 min

D (page 115)

E COMMUNICATE (page 115) 👥

For more practice, go to MyELT.

WATCH ⏱ Time: 40–50 min

F ▶ **1.29** **WATCH FOR MAIN IDEAS** (page 116) Video: 4:17 min

WORDS IN THE TALK

Check understanding of *aneurysm, aorta,* and *buzzword*:

- What might happen to a person with an *aneurysm? (He or she could die.)*
- Which professions work with the *aorta? (doctors, cardiologists, heart surgeons)*
- What are some examples of technology buzzwords? *(smart, disruptive, cutting-edge)*

G THINK CRITICALLY Reflect. (page 116)

H ▶ **1.30** **WATCH FOR DETAILS** (page 116) Video: 1:10 min ☑

Ask students what helped them infer the answer to the first question. *(Seeing the video of the chemistry demonstration followed by Maddie's home video.)*

NOTETAKING SKILL **Use a T-Chart** (page 117)

Tell students that a T-chart is an effective way to compare two things because you can look at them side by side.

I ▶ **1.31** **WATCH AND TAKE NOTES** (page 117) Video: 2:23 min

J COMMUNICATE (page 117)

K THINK CRITICALLY Infer. (page 118) 💡

Explain to students that the words in bold are being used as metaphors. Metaphors explain something by comparing it to something else without using *like* or *as.* Ask students to share any common metaphors about education and learning in their languages.

L ▶ **1.32** **EXPAND YOUR VOCABULARY** (page 118) Video: 2:22 min

M WATCH MORE (page 118)

For more practice, go to MyELT.

AFTER YOU WATCH ⏱ Time: 10–15 min

N REFLECT (page 118) ☑ 👥

Ask students if their intonation will rise or fall at the end of each question in the exercise. *(1. Rise on the first and fall on the second. 2. Fall on both. 3. Rise on the first and fall on the second.)*

EXPANSION Ask students to make a T-chart for their answers to question 2. For example:

SURGEONS VS. TEACHERS	
SIMILARITIES	**DIFFERENCES**
1. *Both work with people.*	1. *Teachers work with the same students, but surgeons don't see the same patients very often.*
2. *Both answer questions from the people they work with.*	2. *Teachers work with many students at the same time while surgeons work with one patient at a time.*

PUT IT TOGETHER ⏱ Time: 10–20 min

A THINK CRITICALLY Synthesize. (page 119)

B THINK CRITICALLY Personalize. (page 119)

COMMUNICATE ⏱ Time: 40–50 min + presentations

> **ASSIGNMENT** **Give an Individual Presentation** about a time when your curiosity led you to learn or try something new. (page 120)
>
> **ALTERNATE ASSIGNMENT** Alternate topic: students choose a typical school subject and present specific ways that teachers could help students become more curious about it.

PREPARE

C (page 120)

> **PRESENTATION SKILL** **Consider Your Audience** (page 120)
>
> Remind students that in class, their classmates are their audience. Ask them to think about the different backgrounds of the other students in the class and answer the four questions about their classmates as an audience.

D ▶ **1.33** (page 121) Video: 0:31 min 💡

E COLLABORATE (page 121)

F (page 121)

PRESENT

G (page 121)

H THINK CRITICALLY Evaluate. (page 121)

> **21C SKILL** Reflect. Ask students to make a T-chart that represents their current presentation skills. The chart can represent their strengths and weaknesses as a presenter.

> **REFLECT BOX** (page 121) Have students play the game "Taboo" to review definitions and synonyms. Students get in pairs. Partner A sits facing the whiteboard, and Partner B sits with back to the whiteboard. To begin the game, write one of the vocabulary words in big letters on the whiteboard. Be sure that all students facing the whiteboard can read the word. Students must remain silent and still until you say, "Go!" When you say, "Go!" Partner A has one minute to get Partner B to say the word or phrase written on the board. Partner A may only use verbal clues and cannot say any part of the vocabulary term. After one minute, students switch seats and roles, and the game repeats.

For more practice, go to MyELT.

THINK AND DISCUSS (page 103)

1. Answers will vary. (E.g., The title expresses what we ask when we are curious about something. Children and researchers usually ask this question.) **2.** Answers will vary. (E.g., Terren might make his sculptures because he's interested in the way electricity looks.)

PART 1

Benefits of Curiosity

A COMMUNICATE (page 104)

1. Answers will vary. (E.g., The child is mixing different colors of paint to make new ones.) **2.** Answers will vary. (E.g., *Curious* means that you want to know more about something. If students are curious about the things they study, they will learn more in school.)

B THINK CRITICALLY Predict. (page 104)

Answers will vary. (E.g., Juan asks if Nancy is a curious person. Nancy answers that she is absolutely curious. She explains that she looks things up on Google every day, and she likes to read Wikipedia, an online encyclopedia. David may or may not say he is a curious person.)

C VOCABULARY (page 105)

1. fascinating **2.** rate **3.** encourages
4. participants **5.** reaction **6.** absolutely
7. involved in **8.** assume **9.** regulates
10. hands-on

D COMMUNICATE (page 106)

Answers will vary.

E LISTEN FOR MAIN IDEAS (page 106)

2., 5.

F LISTEN FOR DETAILS (page 107)

1. a. N, D **b.** D **c.** D **d.** N **e.** J **2.** b

G LISTEN FOR DETAILS (page 107)

1. a. 1 **b.** 3 **c.** 2 **2.** a, c

H MAKING INFERENCES (page 108)

Segment 1

1. T **2.** T **3.** F

Segment 2

4. T **5.** T **6.** F

Segment 3

7. T **8.** T

I THINK CRITICALLY Reflect. (page 109)

Answers will vary.

J (page 109)

1. That's funny. **2.** Oh no! That's awful.
3. How did they study that? **4.** That's fascinating. **5.** Um-hmm…

K COMMUNICATE (page 109)

1. Answers will vary. (E.g., Juan: a smile)
2. Answers will vary. (David: make eye contact; shake head) **3.** Answers will vary. (E.g., Nancy: make eye contact) **4.** Answers will vary. (E.g., David: smile; nod head up and down)
5. Answers will vary. (E.g., Nancy: nod head up and down; make eye contact)

L COMMUNICATE (page 110)

Answers will vary.

M (page 110)

1. rises **2.** falls **3.** rises **4.** rises **5.** falls
6. rises

N COMMUNICATE (page 110)

Answers will vary.

O THINK CRITICALLY Interpret an Infographic. (page 111)

1. Men use Wikipedia more than women. The difference is 6%. **2.** Answers will vary. (E.g., because students have to research a lot at university) **3.** Answers will vary. **4.** Answers will vary.

PART 2 TEDTALKS

3 rules to spark learning

A (page 112)

Answers will vary.

B **COMMUNICATE** (pages 112–113)

Answers will vary.

C **VOCABULARY** (pages 113–114)

1. b **2.** a **3.** c **4.** b **5.** b **6.** b **7.** c
8. c **9.** c **10.** a

D (page 115)

Answers will vary.

E **COMMUNICATE** (page 115)

Answers will vary.

F **WATCH FOR MAIN IDEAS** (page 116)

3.

G **THINK CRITICALLY** Reflect. (page 116)

Answers will vary.

H **WATCH FOR DETAILS** (page 116)

1. b **2.** a **3.** c

I **WATCH AND TAKE NOTES** (page 117)

SURGEON'S RULES	MUSALLAM'S RULES
1. hard	1. Curiosity, Questions
2. Embrace	2. Embrace
3. reflection, revise	3. reflection

J **COMMUNICATE** (page 117)

Answers will vary.

K **THINK CRITICALLY** Infer. (page 118)

1. Answers will vary. (E.g., A magnet is a piece of metal that attracts other metals so that they stick to it. In the talk, Musallam means that questions and curiosity make students interested in what the teachers are saying.)
2. Answers will vary. (E.g., A seed is the tiny bit of a plant that grows into a new plant. In the talk, Musallam means that questions are the starting point that learning grows out of.)   **3.** Answers will vary. (E.g., *Ugly* means "unattractive." We use the word to describe an unattractive person or object. Here Musallam means that the process of learning is messy. It is not simple or organized.)   **4.** Answers will vary. (E.g., Windows allow light to enter a room. Questions allow knowledge to enter the brain.)   **5.** Answers will vary. (E.g., Surgeons ask hard questions and use trial and error to develop the best procedure to save a patient's life. Musallam means that teachers should also ask hard questions and use trial and error to find the best way to teach students.)

L **EXPAND YOUR VOCABULARY** (page 118)

1. a **2.** b **3.** c **4.** b

N **REFLECT** (page 118)

Answers will vary.

PUT IT TOGETHER

A **THINK CRITICALLY** Synthesize. (page 119)

1. Answers will vary. (E.g., Musallam would probably be happy if he were David's father because he understands and appreciates the value of curiosity.)   **2.** Answers will vary. (E.g., Musallam would probably say that this teacher should let Nancy ask as many questions as she wanted to. Questions are an important part of the learning process and show that Nancy was curious.)

B **THINK CRITICALLY** Personalize. (page 119)

Answers will vary.

C (page 120)

Answers will vary.

D (page 121)

Answers will vary. (E.g., Musallam uses *we* because he assumes his audience is made up of other teachers. He also assumes that his listeners understand that "learning is ugly" because they have had the same experiences teaching that he has. To make his talk more interesting, he played video clips that included explosions and several experiments.)

E—REFLECT (page 121)

Answers will vary.

PART 1

Public Space and the Livable City

Listening
Listen for Problems and Solutions

Speaking
Talk about Solutions

Pronunciation
Linking

PART 2

TEDTALKS

Moshe Safdie
How to reinvent the apartment building

Note Taking
Review Your Notes

PUT IT TOGETHER

Communicate
Give an Individual Presentation

Presentation Skill
Organize a Problem-Solution Presentation

UNIT THEME

Unit 7 explores several urban
planning solutions that cities
around the world are using to make
their cities more livable for their
inhabitants.

ACADEMIC TRACK

Urban Planning

UNIT OPENER ⏱ Time: 5–10 min

Ask guiding questions, such as:

- What do you see in the picture? *(flowers and other plants growing on the side of a building; people riding bikes, walking, and running on a large sidewalk)*
- Have you ever seen a building like this? Where?
- Do you think you could grow plants on the side of the building you currently live in?

THINK AND DISCUSS (page 123)

Possible answers:

1. *A "livable city" is one that is comfortable, safe, and pleasant to live in.*
2. *This building could be part of a "livable city" because it provides space to walk and ride bikes and beautiful scenery.*

PART 1

Public Space and the Livable City
▶ **Slideshow available.**

The listening is a lecture in an urban planning class
about how Mérida, in Spain, Seoul, in South Korea,
and Gosford, in Australia, solved some common
city-living problems.

BEFORE YOU LISTEN ⏱ Time: 30–40 min

A COMMUNICATE (page 124)

Read the caption together. Ask students: In
what ways do you think this community is
environmentally-friendly? *(It has a lot of green
space and gardens, space to walk, and windows
to let in light.)*

B 🎧 **2.23** **COLLABORATE** (page 124)
Audio: 0:22 min

VOCABULARY

C 🎧 **2.24** (page 125) Audio: 2:07 min

Have students share if they have been to any of the places mentioned in the vocabulary sentences. Did they like them? Why, or why not?

D COMMUNICATE (page 126)

For more practice, go to MyELT.

LISTEN ⏱ Time: 30–40 min

E 🎧 **2.25** ▶ **1.34** **LISTEN FOR MAIN IDEAS** (page 126) Audio: 3:56 min Video: 3:53 min

> **LISTENING SKILL** **Listen for Problems and Solutions** (page 126)
>
> Explain to students that mind maps (page 87) and T-charts (page 117) are especially effective note-taking skills for when a speaker talks about problems and solutions.

F 🎧 **2.26** **LISTEN FOR DETAILS** (page 127)
Audio: 0:47 min

21C SKILL **Solve Problems.** Working in small groups, have students discuss possible solutions for a place with a lack of fresh food. Encourage them to be creative.

G 🎧 **2.27** **LISTEN FOR DETAILS** (page 127)
Audio: 2:17 min

H COMMUNICATE (page 127)

EXPANSION Ask students if they know of any cities in their home countries that have made specific efforts to be more livable. Have them share this information in small groups, focusing on specific problems and solutions, while the other group members practice listening for and noting problems and solutions.

AFTER YOU LISTEN ⏱ Time: 10–20 min

I THINK CRITICALLY Reflect. (page 128)
Check understanding of the Venn diagram:

- What does the Venn diagram show? *(It compares the characteristics of Factoría Joven, Cheonggyecheon Park, and Gosford Glow Path.)*

- Why do the circles overlap? *(Some of the characteristics are shared by more than one place.)*

For more practice, go to MyELT.

SPEAKING ⏱ Time: 35–45 min

> **SPEAKING SKILL** **Talk about Solutions** (page 129)

For practice with comparative adjectives, go to MyELT.

J THINK CRITICALLY Analyze. (page 129)

K (page 130)

Remind students to vary their language by using different signal words and phrases from the Listening Skill box.

> **PRONUNCIATION SKILL** 🎧 **2.28** **Linking** (page 130) Audio: 0:15 min

L 🎧 **2.29** (page 130) Audio: 0:32 min

Before students listen, have them guess which sounds will be linked by circling them. Then as they listen, they can use lines to connect the sounds that they hear are linked.

M 🎧 **2.30** (page 130) Audio: 0:33 min

N (page 130)

For more practice, go to MyELT.

PART 2 TEDTALKS

How to reinvent the apartment building

MOSHE SAFDIE'S idea worth spreading is that we can plan today for livable cities of the future. We can create apartment buildings and other structures that connect people more closely with each other and with the natural world.

BEFORE YOU WATCH ⏱ Time: 35–45 min

A **THINK CRITICALLY** Predict. (page 131) 💡

Read the quote together and ask students what *this* means. *(building apartment buildings in cities)*

B **COMMUNICATE** (page 132)

EXPANSION Have students work in pairs to create mind maps or T-charts to answer items 2 and 3.

VOCABULARY

C 🎧 **2.31** (pages 132–133) Audio: 2:14 min

D **COMMUNICATE** (page 133)

For more practice, go to MyELT.

WATCH ⏱ Time: 35–45 min

E ▶ **1.35** **WATCH FOR MAIN IDEAS** (page 133)
Video: 2:06 min ✓

Ask students what words the speaker uses to signal the issue and the solution. *(Issue: "we've got to reinvent the apartment building" and "There has to be another way of doing this." Solution: "Let's design a building which gives the qualities of a house to each unit.")*

WORDS IN THE TALK

Check understanding of *prevailing* and *promenades*:

- What is the *prevailing* mood at school?
- How is walking on a *promenade* different from walking on a busy city street? *(It's quieter, prettier, and much more relaxed.)*

F **THINK CRITICALLY** Infer. (page 134) 💡

learn**more** (page 135) Ask students: Do many people live in the suburbs in your home country? How do those people get to work? How good is the public transportation in the suburbs?

G ▶ **1.36** **WATCH FOR DETAILS** (page 135)
Video: 3:24 min

NOTE-TAKING SKILL **Review Your Notes**
(page 136)

H **CHECK YOUR NOTES** (page 136)

I ▶ **1.37** **EXPAND YOUR VOCABULARY**
(page 136) Audio: 2:30 min

J **WATCH MORE** (page 136)

For more practice, go to MyELT.

AFTER YOU WATCH ⏱ Time: 10–20 min

K **THINK CRITICALLY** Infer. (page 136) 💡

L **THINK CRITICALLY** Interpret an Infographic. (page 137) 💡

21C SKILL **Reason Effectively.** Ask students to rate the areas of livability from most important (1) to least important (5). Then, have them discuss why they think the cities on the map became more or less livable.

WORDS IN THE INFOGRAPHIC

Check understanding of *infrastructure* and *stability*:

- What are some problems people might have in a place with poor *infrastructure*? *(a slow and difficult commute, spending money on bottled water, unreliable electricity)*
- What are some problems in a country that does not have *stability*? *(poor economy, protests and demonstrations, war)*

PUT IT TOGETHER ⏱ Time: 15–25 min

A **THINK CRITICALLY** Synthesize.
(page 138) 💡

B **THINK CRITICALLY** Analyze. (page 138) ✓

Encourage students to use the words and phrases they learned in the Listening Skill box as they explain how public spaces, buildings, or other projects can or do solve a community problem.

COMMUNICATE ⏱ Time: 40–50 min + presentations

ASSIGNMENT **Give an Individual Presentation** about a building or public space that makes a city or town more livable. (page 138)

ALTERNATE ASSIGNMENT Have students work as a group or present on a different topic.

- For group presentations, ask the students to work together to present different information. For example, one student could describe the background information for the area, a second could explain the problem, and a third could explain how the building or public space solves that problem.
- Alternate topic: think of a solution to a current problem where you live. Students can refer to the TED Talk to get some ideas of problems and solutions, but should also use their own ideas.

PREPARE

PRESENTATION SKILL **Organize a Problem-Solution Presentation** (page 139)

C COLLABORATE (page 139)

D (pages 139–140)

E PRACTICE (page 141)

F (page 141)

PREPARE

G (page 141)

Have students take notes on one presentation. Assign at least two people to take notes on the same presentation. They should check their notes with each other after the presentation, and add anything they missed in a different color. Collect these to check students' ability to review their notes.

H THINK CRITICALLY Evaluate. (page 141)

REFLECT BOX (page 141) Have students sort the words by part of speech to review usage. Remind them to reference vocabulary exercises in Parts 1 and 2 to understand the words in context.
- *Adjectives: affordable, attractive, middle-income, public*
- *Adverbs: extremely*
- *Nouns: concept, density, pedestrian, performance space, recreation, resident, sewer, unit*
- *Verbs: draw, hang out, integrate with, lead, reconfigure, rethink, sustain*

For more practice, go to MyELT.

THINK AND DISCUSS (page 123)

1. Answers will vary (E.g., A "livable city" is one that is comfortable to live in.)   **2.** Answers will vary. (E.g., This building looks like part of a "livable city" because it provides beautiful scenery and space to walk and ride bikes.)

PART 1

Public Space and the Livable City

A COMMUNICATE (page 124)

Answers will vary.

B COLLABORATE (page 124)

Answers will vary.

C VOCABULARY (page 125)

1. pedestrians   **2.** draw   **3.** attractive   **4.** hang out   **5.** recreation   **6.** performance center   **7.** residents   **8.** public   **9.** lead   **10.** sewer

D COMMUNICATE (page 126)

Answers will vary.

E LISTEN FOR MAIN IDEAS (page 126)

3.

F LISTEN FOR DETAILS (page 127)

1. c   **2.** a   **3.** d

G LISTEN FOR DETAILS (page 127)

Factoria Joven: a, d, f
Cheonggyecheon Park: b, e, i
Gosford Glow Footpath: c, g, h

H COMMUNICATE (page 127)

Answers will vary.

I THINK CRITICALLY Reflect. (page 128)

1. Answers will vary. (E.g., All: a, c)
2. Answers will vary. (E.g., Factoria Joven & Cheonggyecheon Park: b. Cheonggyecheon Park & Gosford Glow Footpath: d, g)

3. Answers will vary. (E.g., Cheonggyecheon Park: e. Gosford Glow Footpath: f)
4. Answers will vary.

J THINK CRITICALLY Analyze. (page 129)

Answers will vary.

K (page 130)

Answers will vary.

L (page 130)

1. "se" and "a" in *these are*   **2.** "s" and "a" in *It's attractive*   **3.** "t" and "a" in *It attracts*; "s" and "a" in *attracts about*; "le" and "ea" in *people each*   **4.** "ke" and "a" in *take a*; "k" and "a" in *look at*; "me" and "ex" in *some examples*   **5.** "y" and "a" in *They also*; "ve" and "o" in *solve other*; "s" and "o" in *problems of*

M (page 130)

1. It's in   **2.** That's on   **3.** look at   **4.** an open   **5.** path at

N (page 130)

See answers for L and M.

PART 2 **TED**TALKS

How to reinvent the apartment building

A THINK CRITICALLY Predict. (page 131)

Answers will vary. (E.g., Safdie wants to reinvent apartment buildings to help people connect to nature when they live in big, crowded cities. Apartments don't have a lot of natural light, open space, or gardens, and he wants to change that.)

B COMMUNICATE (page 132)

Answers will vary.

C VOCABULARY (pages 132–133)

1. b   **2.** c   **3.** b   **4.** b   **5.** a   **6.** a   **7.** c   **8.** b   **9.** a   **10.** c

D COMMUNICATE (page 133)

Answers will vary.

E WATCH FOR MAIN IDEAS (page 133)

Issue: 2.
Solution: 3.

F THINK CRITICALLY Infer. (page 134)

1. Answers will vary. (E.g., He's describing people who do not have a lot of money.)
2. Answers will vary. (E.g., They have no choice because they can only live in places that are not expensive.)

G WATCH FOR DETAILS (page 135)

1. apartments   2. community   3. garden
4. light   5. incomes   6. three hours
7. incomes   8. community   9. parks
10. urban   11. public   12. longest

H CHECK YOUR NOTES (page 136)

Answers will vary.

I EXPAND YOUR VOCABULARY (page 136)

1. a   2. a   3. c   4. b

K THINK CRITICALLY Infer. (page 136)

1. Answers will vary. (E.g., The suburbs are very spread out. You have to drive everywhere. This isn't good for the environment, and it uses up resources.)   2. Answers will vary. (E.g., Houses have space around them. They have gardens and places for children to play. They have more privacy than apartments.)

L THINK CRITICALLY Interpret an Infographic. (page 137)

1. 2010 and 2015   2. Detroit, US; Paris, France; Tripoli, Libya; Kiev, Ukraine; Damascus, Syria   3. Honolulu, US; Kathmandu, Nepal; Harare, Zimbabwe   4. Australia   5. stability, infrastructure, education, health care, environment

PUT IT TOGETHER

A THINK CRITICALLY Synthesize. (page 138)

1. Answers will vary. (E.g., Provide places for young people to hang out, such as Factoria Joven; create places for people to enjoy nature, such as Cheonggyecheon Park; make places safer and more attractive, such as Gosford Glow Path; build apartments that have space around them, lots of light, and that bring people together, like Habitat.)   2. Answers will vary.

B THINK CRITICALLY Analyze. (page 138)

Answers will vary.

C COLLABORATE (page 139)

Answers will vary.

D—REFLECT (pages 139–141)

Answers will vary.

UNIT 8 Life Lessons

PART 1
How to Change Your Life

Note Taking
Record Definitions

Listening
Listen for Listing Words and Phrases

Speaking
Rephrase Key Ideas

Pronunciation
Vowels in Unstressed Syllables

PART 2
TEDTALKS

Ric Elias
3 things I learned while my plane crashed

PUT IT TOGETHER

Communicate
Give an Individual Presentation

Presentation Skill
Have a Strong Conclusion

UNIT THEME

Unit 8 explores ways of making changes that positively impact our lives, and the importance of learning from our life experiences.

ACADEMIC TRACK

Psychology

UNIT OPENER Time: 5–10 min

Ask guiding questions, such as:

- What is the setting of this picture? *(a backyard)*
- Why do you think these people are dressed in such fancy clothes? *(They are getting ready to go somewhere special. They want to make an ordinary day feel special.)*

THINK AND DISCUSS (page 143)

Possible answers:

1. Life lessons *are important information that people learn through experience.*
2. *They feel happy and don't have any worries. They have probably learned that life is short, and to enjoy every moment.*

PART 1

How to Change Your Life
▶ **Slideshow available.**

The listening is a lecture in a psychology class about how to make positive changes in your life.

BEFORE YOU LISTEN ◑ Time: 30–40 min

A COMMUNICATE (page 144) 👥

Before the students start the exercise, have them cover the caption and guess what it says. How might the image relate to making changes in your life? *(Change is challenging. Change can physically and mentally affect you.)*

B 🎧 2.32 COLLABORATE (page 144)
Audio: 0:32 min

VOCABULARY

C (page 145)
Have students work in small groups. If no one in the group knows the definition to a word, then the group should look it up in a dictionary.

For practice with Verb + infinitive, go to MyELT.

D 🎧 **2.33** (page 145) Audio: 1:20 min

Remind students that they may need to change the form of the word to complete these sentences.

E COMMUNICATE (page 146)

For more practice, go to MyELT.

LISTEN 🕐 Time: 30–40 min

F 🎧 **2.34** ▶ **1.38** **LISTEN FOR MAIN IDEAS** (page 146) Audio: 3:55 min Video: 3:56 min

> **NOTE-TAKING SKILL** Record Definitions (page 147)
>
> Tell students that recording definitions will not only help them to remember the content of a lecture, but will also help them remember new vocabulary.

G 🎧 **2.35** **LISTEN FOR DETAILS** (page 147)
Audio: 1:44 min

> **LISTENING SKILL** Listen for Listing Words and Phrases (page 147)
>
> Remind students that they learned about listing signals in the Speaking Skill box on page 48.

H 🎧 **2.36** (page 148) Audio: 1:56 min

I (page 148)

AFTER YOU LISTEN 🕐 Time: 10–15 min

J THINK CRITICALLY Personalize. (page 149)

> **21C SKILL** Reflect. Ask students to make a list of things that they do because of intrinsic motivation and a list of things they do because of extrinsic motivation. Then ask them to explain which things are more important to them (likely things they do because of intrinsic motivation), and if they can think of any intrinsic motivations for doing some of the things on the list that are currently extrinsically motivated.

For more practice, go to MyELT.

SPEAKING 🕐 Time: 45–55 min

> **SPEAKING SKILL** Rephrase Key Ideas (page 149)
>
> Point out that learning to identify when a speaker is rephrasing key ideas can aid in listening comprehension.

K (page 149)

L COLLABORATE (page 150)

> **PRONUNCIATION SKILL** 🎧 **2.37** Vowels in Unstressed Syllables (page 150)
> Audio: 0:17 min
>
> Point out that the unstressed vowel in each of these words is different to highlight the fact that any vowel can be reduced to the schwa sound.

M 🎧 **2.38** (page 150) Audio: 0:38 min

Before listening to the audio, have students try to guess which syllable has the schwa sound by figuring out which is the unstressed syllable and circling it. Then they can underline the unstressed syllables they hear as they listen to the audio.

N (page 150)

O COMMUNICATE (page 150)

P (page 151)

Q (page 151)

For more practice, go to MyELT.

PART 2 TEDTALKS

3 things I learned while my plane crashed

RIC ELIAS'S idea worth spreading is that life can change in an instant, so don't delay. Be the best person you can be right now.

BEFORE YOU WATCH 🕐 Time: 30–40 min

A THINK CRITICALLY Predict. (page 152)

Read the quote together, and ask students what *it* means. (Life)

B COMMUNICATE (page 152)

VOCABULARY

C 🎧 2.39 (page 153) Audio: 2:00 min

D COMMUNICATE (page 154)

For more practice, go to MyELT.

WATCH ⏱ Time: 35–45 min

E ▶ 1.39 **WATCH FOR MAIN IDEAS** (page 154)
Video: 4:54 min

WORDS IN THE TALK

Check understanding of *brace for impact* and *clear something:*

- What do you do with your body when you *brace for impact? (curl into a ball, cover your head with your arms)*
- What might happen if a vehicle doesn't *clear* an object above or below it? *(It will crash.)*

> learn**more** (page 154) Ask students: Have there been any dramatic accidents and survival stories in your home country recently? If so, what happened?

F THINK CRITICALLY Infer. (page 155) 💡

G ▶ 1.40 **WATCH FOR DETAILS** (page 155)
Video: 1:39 min

H ▶ 1.41 **LISTEN FOR LISTING WORDS**
(page 155) Video: 3:05 min ☑

Review listening for listing words and phrases. Ask students what listing words or phrases the speaker uses for each lesson. *(1: no listing word or phrase; 2. "The second thing I learned…"; 3. "The third thing I learned…")*

I ▶ 1.41 **WATCH FOR DETAILS**
(pages 155–156) Video: 3:05 min

J ▶ 1.42 **WATCH FOR REPHRASING**
(page 156) Video: 0:32 min

K ▶ 1.43 **EXPAND YOUR VOCABULARY**
(page 156) Video: 2:04 min

L WATCH MORE (page 156)

For more practice, go to MyELT.

AFTER YOU WATCH ⏱ Time: 40–50 min

M COMMUNICATE (page 156)
EXPANSION Have students use the questions to conduct a survey of people outside the class. Each student should survey five people, and then share their results with the class. What similarities and differences are there in people's responses?

N THINK CRITICALLY Interpret an Infographic.
(page 157) 💡

Check understanding of the infographic:

- What is shown? *(a comparison of what men and women have on their bucket lists)*
- What are the bucket list items? *(things men and women hope to do in their lives)*

O (page 158)

P (page 158)

Q (page 158)

R (page 158)
EXPANSION Ask students to compare their class list to the infographic on page 157. Do the men and women in the class have similar things on their bucket list as the men and women in the infographic? How are they the same or different?

PUT IT TOGETHER ⏱ Time: 15–20 min

A THINK CRITICALLY Synthesize. (page 159) 💡

B THINK CRITICALLY Personalize.
(page 159)

COMMUNICATE 🕐 Time: 40–50 min + presentations

> **ASSIGNMENT** **Give an Individual Presentation** about a change you made or that you want to make. (page 159)
>
> **ALTERNATE ASSIGNMENT** Have students work as a group to present specific steps people can take to learn English.

PREPARE

> **PRESENTATION SKILL** **Have a Strong Conclusion** (page 159)
>
> Remind students that the conclusion is the last thing their audience will hear. It is their last chance, as a speaker, to emphasize any key points, to remind the audience what was important about the presentation, and to give the audience something specific to think about or do. Presentations should end purposefully. Having a specific ending in mind can also help you remember what to say at the end of a presentation.

C (page 160)

D COLLABORATE (page 161)

E (page 161)

PRESENT

F (page 161)

G THINK CRITICALLY Evaluate. (page 161)

> **REFLECT BOX** (page 161) Have students play a quick word association game to review the meanings of the vocabulary words. In pairs, have students sit facing each other. Partner A says a word from the vocabulary list, and Partner B says the first word he or she associates with the chosen word. The association can be any part of speech, a synonym or antonym, or even a specific name or brand. For example, the vocabulary word *accomplish* could associate with *achieve, finish, fail (antonym), motivation, or goal*. The vocabulary word *avoid* could associate with *stay away, do (antonym), dislike, unpleasant,* and *unhealthy*. After Partner B makes the association, Partner A immediately chooses a new word from the list and repeats the task. When Partner B has made associations for all the vocabulary words, partners switch roles.

For more practice, go to MyELT.

THINK AND DISCUSS (page 143)

1. Answers will vary. (E.g., *Life lessons* are important information that people learn through experience.) **2.** Answers will vary. (E.g., They feel happy and don't have any worries. They have probably learned that life is short, and to enjoy every moment.)

PART 1

How to Change Your Life

A COMMUNICATE (page 144)

Answers will vary.

B COLLABORATE (page 144)

Answers will vary. (E.g., The students answer that people often want to eat healthier food, get along better with family, be a better student, and get to class on time. Other examples of changes people often want to make include: getting in shape, spending less time on social media, being more social, getting better grades, spending less money, etc.)

C VOCABULARY (page 145)

1. d **2.** h **3.** j **4.** f **5.** e **6.** b **7.** i **8.** a
9. c **10.** g

D (page 145)

1. factor **2.** desire **3.** reward **4.** avoid
5. punishment **6.** behavior **7.** Experts
8. principles **9.** accomplish **10.** reinforce

E COMMUNICATE (page 146)

Answers will vary.

F LISTEN FOR MAIN IDEAS (page 146)

2., 5.

G LISTEN FOR DETAILS (page 147)

1. the desire to do things **2.** outside, reward, avoid **3.** inside, enjoyable

H (page 148)

1. Second **2.** Finally **3.** First

I (page 148)

Principle 1: c

Principle 2: b

Principle 3: a

J THINK CRITICALLY Personalize. (page 149)

Answers will vary.

K (page 149)

1. check above *That is*; underline *People who have intrinsic motivation do things for their own sake*; two lines under *they do a thing because the thing itself is a reward* **2.** check above *In other words*; underline *This helps reinforce a new behavior*; two lines under *it helps to make a new behavior a habit* **3.** underline *You need to enjoy the process of change*; two lines under *Find pleasure in the new behavior*

L COLLABORATE (page 150)

Answers will vary.

M (page 150)

1. a - void **2.** oc - cur **3.** sup - port
4. prob - lem **5.** meth – od **6.** sys – tem
7. pro - vide **8.** com - pare

N (page 150)

See answers for exercise M

O COMMUNICATE (page 150)

Answers will vary.

P (page 151)

Answers will vary.

Q (page 151)

Answers will vary.

PART 2 TEDTALKS

3 things I learned while my plane crashed

A THINK CRITICALLY Predict. (page 152)

Answers will vary. (E.g., a story about a person who survived a plane crash; lessons a person learned from being in a plane crash)

B COMMUNICATE (page 152)

Answers will vary.

C VOCABULARY (page 153)

1. h **2.** i **3.** e **4.** a **5.** c **6.** f **7.** j **8.** d
9. g **10.** b

D COMMUNICATE (page 154)

Answers will vary.

E WATCH FOR MAIN IDEAS (page 154)

1., **3.**

F THINK CRITICALLY Infer. (page 155)

Answers will vary. (E.g., Elias didn't need any more information from the flight attendants because he knew what was going to happen.)

G WATCH FOR DETAILS (page 155)

Elias's plane takes off → d → b→ e→ a→ c → Pilot says "Brace for impact."

H LISTEN FOR LISTING WORDS (page 155)

3. Dying isn't scary, it's just sad. **2.** Don't waste your time on things that don't matter.
1. Don't postpone anything.

I WATCH FOR DETAILS (pages 155–156)

Lesson 1

1. change **2.** people, experiences **2.** urgency

Lesson 2

1. regretted, doing things **2.** reflected on, eliminate **3.** happy

Lesson 3

1. scared **2.** loved **3.** wish

J WATCH FOR REPHRASING (page 156)

1. things we want to do in life **2.** no

K EXPAND YOUR VOCABULARY (page 156)

1. b **2.** b **3.** b **4.** a

M COMMUNICATE (page 156)

Answers will vary.

N THINK CRITICALLY Interpret an Infographic. (page 157)

1. Travel more **2.** Go skydiving **3.** Climb a mountain **4.** Propose/Get married **5.** women

O (page 158)

Answers will vary.

P (page 158)

Answers will vary.

Q (page 158)

Answers will vary.

R (page 158)

Answers will vary.

PUT IT TOGETHER

A THINK CRITICALLY Synthesize. (page 159)

1. Answers will vary. (E.g., The professor is talking about changes you make thoughtfully. A dramatic event led Elias to make changes.
2. Answers will vary. (E.g., He may have to reinforce his behaviors because they are new. However, he has a strong motivation to change so he may not need a lot of reinforcement.)

B THINK CRITICALLY Personalize. (page 159)

Answers will vary.

C—REFLECT (pages 160–161)

Answers will vary.

Audio Scripts

Unit 1

AUDIO TRACK 1.2 1:41 min

Part 1, Page 5, Exercise C, Vocabulary

a. Australia is very rich in natural **resources**, including coal, copper, iron, gold, and uranium.

b. One way to **conserve** electricity is to turn off the lights when you leave a room.

c. Each month, the government publishes **statistics** about the number of people who found and lost jobs.

d. You shouldn't use the dishwasher when it is only half full because it **wastes** water.

e. I probably drink eight glasses of water a day **on average**; some days I drink more and some days less.

f. When I moved to an apartment near my job, I **cut** my driving time from 30 minutes to 10 minutes.

g. Lake Ontario is **huge**. It looks like an ocean!

h. The professor **requires** students to turn off their cell phones in his class.

i. There's water on the bathroom floor. I think the bathtub has a **leak**.

j. It's **crucial** to drink water after you exercise. Your body needs it.

AUDIO TRACK 1.3 3:41 min

Page 6, Exercise E, Listen for Main Ideas

HARRY Good afternoon, this is Daily Report and I'm Harry Martinez. Well, today is March 22nd, United Nations World Water Day. And here to talk to us about how we can save this important natural resource is Chandra Cassidy, general manager of the department of water and power. Welcome, Ms. Cassidy.

CHANDRA Thank you very much.

HARRY So first of all, why is it important for everyone, not just people in dry places, to **conserve** water?

CHANDRA It's important for two reasons. One obvious reason is to save money. Lots of people have very high water bills each month because they use too much water. But more importantly, the world doesn't have enough fresh water. Here are some statistics for your viewers to think about. Water covers 70 percent of the earth, but less than 2 percent is fresh water, water that we can drink. And the world's population is growing. Right now we have almost 7.5 billion people on earth. In thirty years it's going to be 9 billion. Where will we find enough water for all those people?

HARRY Right. So what should people do to save water in their homes? Can you give us some tips?

CHANDRA Sure. Let's start with a really easy one. Don't run the water when you brush your teeth. If you leave the water running, it wastes two and a half gallons of water a minute.

HARRY That's a lot of wasted water. And money.

CHANDRA Yeah, and next, here's another easy one. Take shorter showers. Do you take a shower every day?

HARRY Yes...

CHANDRA How long is your shower, on average?

HARRY I don't know, eight minutes? Ten minutes?

CHANDRA So try to cut your shower time from eight minutes to just five minutes. If you do that, you can save 25 gallons each time you take a shower.

HARRY 25 gallons! That's a lot!

CHANDRA And here's one more tip. Don't eat meat. Or eat less meat. Most people never think about this. It takes a huge amount of water to produce meat. For example, it takes 1,799 gallons of water to produce just one pound of beef.

HARRY Wow, really? Why?

CHANDRA Because you have to feed and take care of the cow for years before you can eat it. And that requires a lot of water.

HARRY I never thought of that before. Anything else?

CHANDRA Yes. Fix leaky faucets. It's crucial to do this because even a small leak can waste a lot of water. In fact, leaks waste more than 3,000 gallons of water a year. That's more than 13 percent of all the water we use.

HARRY Well, thank you for these tips, Chandra. We need to take a break now, but before we go, what message would you like to leave our viewers with?

CHANDRA Well, the main message is that small changes can make a big difference. You can help the environment and save money if you follow these simple suggestions for conserving water.

AUDIO TRACK 1.4 2:08 min

Page 7, Exercise F, Listen for Details

Segment 1

HARRY So first of all why is it important for everyone, not just people in dry places, to conserve water?

CHANDRA It's important for two reasons. One obvious reason is to save money. Lots of people have very high water bills each month because they use too much water. But more importantly, the world doesn't have enough fresh water. Here are some statistics for your viewers to think about. Water covers 70 percent of the earth, but less than 2 percent is fresh water, water that we can drink. And the world's population is growing. Right now we have almost 7.5 billion people on earth. In thirty years it's going to be 9 billion. Where will we find enough water for all those people?

Segment 2

CHANDRA And here's one more tip. Don't eat meat. Or eat less meat. Most people never think about this. It takes a huge amount of water to produce meat. For example, it takes 1,799 gallons of water to produce just one pound of beef.

HARRY Wow, really? Why?

CHANDRA Because you have to feed and take care of the cow for years before you can eat it. And that requires a lot of water.

HARRY I never thought of that before. Anything else?

CHANDRA Yes. Fix leaky faucets. It's crucial to do this because even a small leak can waste a lot of water. In fact, leaks waste more than 3,000 gallons of water a year. That's more than 13 percent of all the water we use.

AUDIO TRACK 1.5 2:01 min

Page 8, Exercise G

Segment 3

HARRY Right. So what should people do to save water in their homes? Can you give us some tips?

CHANDRA Sure. Let's start with a really easy one. Don't run the water when you brush your teeth. If you leave the water running, it wastes two and a half gallons of water a minute.

HARRY That's a lot of wasted water. And money.

CHANDRA Yeah, and next, here's another easy one. Take shorter showers. Do you take a shower every day?

HARRY Yes…

CHANDRA How long is your shower, on average?

HARRY I don't know, 8 minutes? 10 minutes?

CHANDRA So try to cut your shower time from 8 minutes to just five minutes. if you do that, you can save 25 gallons each time you take a shower.

HARRY 25 gallons! That's a lot!

CHANDRA And here's one more tip. Don't eat meat. Or eat less meat. Most people never think about this. It takes a huge amount of water to produce meat. For example, it takes 1,799 gallons of water to produce just one pound of beef.

HARRY Wow, really? Why?

CHANDRA Because you have to feed and take care of the cow for years before you can eat it. And that requires a lot of water.

HARRY I never thought of that before. Anything else?

CHANDRA Yes. Fix leaky faucets. It's crucial to do this because even a small leak can waste a lot of water. In fact, leaks waste more than 3,000 gallons of water a year. That's more than 13 percent of all the water we use.

AUDIO TRACK 1.6 0:19 min

Page 10, Pronunciation Skill: Syllable Stress

Two syllables: water

Three syllables: natural

Four syllables: environment

AUDIO TRACK 1.7 0:26 min

Page 11, Exercise L

conserving	enough	statistics	leaky
percent	population	suggestions	wasted

AUDIO TRACK 1.8 1:30 min

Part 2, page 13, Exercise C, Vocabulary

1. I used a calculator to add the long list of **figures**.
2. Don't throw your paper in the trash; **recycle** it instead.
3. Our gas bill is huge! We need to **reduce** the amount of energy we use each month.
4. When the paper towel comes out of an automatic machine, you need to **tear** it **off** before you can use it.
5. Please take the rug outside and **shake** it to remove the dust.
6. After I do my laundry, I **fold** my clothes and put them in the drawer.
7. I think the smartphone is the most amazing **invention** of the 21st century.

8. I waved to my friend in the parking lot, but she didn't see me.
9. After he washed his hands, Bob dried them with a paper towel from the **dispenser** on the wall.
10. The medical tests proved that my uncle did not have cancer.

Unit 2

AUDIO TRACK 1.9 0:31 min

Part 1, page 24, Exercise B, Think Critically, Predict

SHARON Hey Tom! Welcome back! How was your vacation?

TOM It was … awesome.

SHARON Oh yeah? Where did you go?

TOM I went to the Serengeti National Park. I spent ten days on a photo safari.

SHARON Wow! What made you decide to do that?

TOM Well, there were a couple of reasons.

AUDIO TRACK 1.10 1:29 min

Page 25, Exercise C, Vocabulary

a. Gayle and **a couple of** her friends decided to go camping, so they bought a tent for three people.
b. Tigers are **endangered** animals. We have to protect them before they disappear.
c. The **landscape** was flat and brown, with low hills in the distance.
d. My dog **chases** every cat he sees, but he never catches them.
e. There are only about 800 mountain gorillas in the world today. They are in serious danger of becoming **extinct**.
f. The seasons follow each other in an endless **cycle**.
g. The Amazon jungle is getting smaller because of human activity. **Conservation** is necessary to protect it.
h. If you're going to hike in the desert, it is **essential** to take lots of water with you.
i. The law protects elephants in Africa, but each day hunters kill hundreds of them **illegally**.
j. Akiko wants to get into the best university, so she has a strong **motivation** to study hard.

AUDIO TRACK 1.11 4:01 min

Page 26, Exercise E, Listen for Main Ideas and page 27, Exercise F, Listen for Details

SHARON Hey Tom! Welcome back! How was your vacation?

TOM It was … awesome.

SHARON Oh yeah? Where did you go?

TOM I went to the Serengeti National Park. I spent ten days on a photo safari.

SHARON Wow! What made you decide to do that?

TOM Well, there were a couple of reasons.

TOM First of all, about six months ago I read an article called something like "Why you should go on a safari to Africa, NOW." The main point was that countries like Kenya and Tanzania rely on tourism to pay for wildlife conservation. And conservation is essential because so many African animals are endangered. For example, there used to be about 65,000 black rhinos in Arica. And now there are only about 4,000 in the whole world. They're almost extinct.

SHARON Really?! What happened to them?

TOM Poaching! People killing them illegally! I decided that if I could help to save rhinos or elephants or any other animals by going on a safari, I was going to do it. That was my main motivation.

SHARON I see. What was the other reason?

TOM Well, you know that I love photography.

SHARON Oh yeah, how many pictures did you take?

TOM About a thousand.

SHARON Oo, can I see them?

TOM Well I only have a few here, but sure. Let's see… OK, here's a typical Serengeti landscape.

SHARON Wait, how big is the Serengeti?

TOM It covers five thousand seven hundred square miles. You can see how flat it is. It's just miles and miles of tall grass, and here and there you see acacia trees, you know, the famous ones that look like umbrellas.

SHARON It's so green.

TOM Yeah, April is the rainy season. It rained every day on my trip.

SHARON Did you travel alone, or did you go with a guide?

TOM I went on a group tour with a professional guide. We traveled in jeeps with seven seats and at night we slept in tents, in a camp.

SHARON That sounds like fun.

TOM Yeah, it was. Here's a picture I took at a drinking hole early one morning.

SHARON I see zebra and… what are these black animals with horns?

TOM They're called wildebeests. They're members of the antelope family. They look kind of scary, don't you think?

SHARON Yeah. Uh, what about the big cats, you know, lions, cheetahs, leopards? Did you see any of those?

TOM No leopards, but lots of lions. Here, look. One afternoon we were driving along and we saw these two female lions lying in the middle of the road, asleep. So our guide stopped the jeep about ten feet away and we just sat there watching them for about fifteen minutes. They never moved.

SHARON Aw, nice picture.

TOM And here's a shot of a female cheetah. She's chasing a baby gazelle, see? The Serengeti has around one thousand five hundred cheetahs. That's the second largest cheetah population in Africa.

SHARON Cheetahs are the fastest land animals, right?

TOM Right.

SHARON That's a great photo. What happened to the gazelle?

TOM The cheetah caught it about 30 seconds after I took this picture.

SHARON Oh no! How did it make you feel to see that?

TOM I … accepted it. See, when you're out there in the park, you realize how everything in nature is connected. Animals like gazelles eat grass and then animals like cheetahs eat gazelles. That's how nature works. It's an endless cycle, and we're just a tiny part of it.

AUDIO TRACK 1.12 0:28 min

Page 27, Listening Skill: Recognize a Speaker's Tone and Feeling

SHARON Hey Tom! Welcome back! How was your vacation?

TOM It was … awesome.

SHARON Oh yeah? Where did you go?

TOM I went to the Serengeti National Park. I spent ten days on a photo safari.

SHARON Wow! What made you decide to do that?

AUDIO TRACK 1.13 1:36 min

Page 28, Exercise G

1.

TOM [T]here used to be about 65,000 black rhinos in Arica. And now there are only about 4,000 in the whole world. They're almost extinct.

SHARON Really?! What happened to them?

2.

SHARON Really?! What happened to them?

TOM Poaching! People killing them illegally! I decided that if I could help to save rhinos or elephants or any other animals by going on a safari, I was going to do it. That was my main motivation.

3.

TOM Well, you know that I love photography.

SHARON Oh yeah, how many pictures did you take?

TOM About a thousand.

4.

SHARON Cheetahs are the fastest land animals, right?

TOM Right.

SHARON That's a great photo. What happened to the gazelle?

TOM The cheetah caught it about 30 seconds after I took this picture.

SHARON Oh no! How did it make you feel to see that?

5.

SHARON Oh no! How did it make you feel to see that?

TOM I … accepted it. See, when you're out there in the park, you realize how everything in nature is connected. Animals like gazelles eat grass and then animals like cheetahs eat gazelles. That's how nature works. It's an endless cycle, and we're just a tiny part of it.

AUDIO TRACK 1.14 0:55 min

Page 29, Exercise I

Segment 1

SHARON Did you travel alone, or did you go with a guide?

TOM I went on a group tour with a professional guide. We traveled in jeeps with seven seats and at night we slept in tents, in a camp.

SHARON That sounds like fun.

Segment 2

SHARON What about the big cats, you know, lions, cheetahs, leopards? Did you see any of those?

TOM No leopards, but lots of lions. Here, look. One afternoon we were driving along and we saw these two female lions lying in the middle of the road, asleep. So our guide stopped the jeep about ten feet away and we just sat there watching them for about fifteen minutes. They never moved.

AUDIO TRACK 1.15 0:14 min

Page 29, Pronunciation Skill: Thought Groups and Pausing

Hey Tom! Welcome back! How was your vacation?

AUDIO TRACK 1.16 1:18 min

Page 29, Exercise K and page 30, Exercise L

1. The main point was that countries like Kenya and Tanzania rely on tourism to pay for wildlife conservation.
2. It covers five thousand seven hundred square miles.
3. Here's a picture I took at a drinking hole early one morning.
4. They're members of the antelope family. They look kind of scary, don't you think?
5. One afternoon we were driving along and we saw these two female lions lying in the middle of the road, asleep.
6. So our guide stopped the jeep about ten feet away, and we just sat there watching them for about 15 minutes.
7. Animals like gazelles eat grass and then animals like cheetahs eat gazelles.

AUDIO TRACK 1.17 1:38 min

Part 2, page 34, Exercise D, Vocabulary

1. Bees and flowers are **interconnected**. One cannot live without the other one.
2. While working in the hot sun, I **perspired** so much that my shirt got all wet.
3. The photos and diagrams **illustrate** how clouds form.
4. A tornado is so powerful that it **is capable of** lifting cars and throwing them in the air.
5. Even from a distance of five miles, the tornado was a **spectacular** sight.
6. The tornado travelled in a **straight** line for 10 miles, and then it turned suddenly in a different direction.
7. Last summer, Tim **witnessed** a tornado for the first time. "It was a sight I will never forget," he said.
8. Millions of years ago, powerful **forces** pushed up the earth and created the Rocky Mountains.
9. Planting a vegetable garden is a simple **process** with easy-to-follow instructions.
10. The universe probably includes millions of **planets** like our Earth.

Unit 3

AUDIO TRACK 1.18 0:48 min

Part 1, page 44, Exercise B, Communicate and page 46, Listening Skill: Listen for Signposts

JEAN Hi everybody. Thanks for attending our panel discussion. Let's start with a little survey. How many of you came to school by private car today? Eleven! Well as you know, a car is not a very ecofriendly method of transportation. Today we're going to talk about three alternative methods that are ecofriendly, fast, and efficient. Miguel will speak first.

AUDIO TRACK 1.19 1:34 min

Page 45, Exercise C, Vocabulary

a. "Hello. I'm taking a **survey** about transportation. Can I ask you some questions?"
b. This sports car has a powerful engine. It has the capacity to go from 0 to 100 miles per hour in 30 seconds.

c. The newest electric cars have a **range** of about 200 miles before the battery dies.
d. The weather report says there is a 100 percent chance of snow tonight. I definitely won't ride my bike to work tomorrow.
e. Public transportation is a **convenient** way to get to work, because you don't have to worry about parking.
f. To get downtown, there are several **alternatives**. You can take the subway, the trolley, or a bus.
g. The street is very **narrow**. There isn't enough room for two cars to pass.
h. My cell phone is almost dead. I need to **charge** the battery.
i. The building has a complicated security **system**. It uses many types of locks, gates, and cameras.
j. One **benefit** of riding my bike to work is that I don't have to waste time waiting for a bus.

AUDIO TRACK 1.20 0:45 min

Page 47, Exercise E, Listen for Main Ideas

MIGUEL Hi everyone. To begin, I want to tell you about a very unusual method of transportation in La Paz, the biggest city in my country, Bolivia. It is called Mi Teleférico, which means "my cable car."

JEAN Thank you, Miguel. Now it's my turn. I'm going to present a type of transportation that's becoming more and more popular all over the world, especially in my country, China—electric bicycles, or ebikes.

YULIA Thank you, Jean. My topic today is electric microcars

AUDIO TRACK 1.21 2:09 min

Page 47, Exercise F, Listen for Details

Segment 1

JEAN Hi everybody. Thanks for attending our panel discussion. Let's start with a little survey. How many of you came to school by private car today? Eleven! Well as you know, a car is not a very ecofriendly method of transportation.

Today we're going to talk about three alternative methods that are ecofriendly, fast, and efficient. Miguel will speak first.

MIGUEL Hi everyone. To begin, I want to tell you about a very unusual method of transportation in La Paz, the biggest city in my country, Bolivia. It is called Mi Teleférico, which means "my cable car." La Paz is in a valley with mountains all around. About 200,000 people live in another small city at the top of the mountain called El Alto. In the past, these people had to travel up and down the mountain by bus or car to get to work. It took a long time, it was dangerous, and all the cars caused a lot of noise, traffic, and pollution.

My city built Mi Teleférico as a solution to these problems. The system opened in 2014 with three lines, and there are plans for six more lines by 2019. Right now it has the capacity to carry 600 passengers per day.

The system has some important benefits for my city. First, a cable car leaves the station every 12 seconds, so it's very convenient. Second, it's fast. It can take passengers from El Alto to La Paz, a distance of about 4 miles, in about 13 minutes. Another plus is that it's cheap; it costs about 40 cents to travel each way. And finally, the system is ecofriendly since it uses electricity.

AUDIO TRACK 1.22 1:22 min

Page 48, Exercise G, Listen for Details

Segment 2

JEAN Thank you, Miguel. Now it's my turn. I'm going to present a type of transportation that's becoming more and more popular all over the world, especially in my country, China—electric bicycles, or ebikes. An ebike is basically a regular bike with a motor and a battery. It's useful, for example, if you're going up a hill.

Most ebikes can easily travel 20 to 30 miles per hour. The battery range is about 18 miles, which is enough for most people to get to and from work. In the United States a basic electric bike costs between a thousand and fifteen hundred dollars. Maybe that's a lot for a bicycle, but after that it's very cheap to operate. It only costs about 15 cents to charge; that's less than a penny per mile. It's three times less expensive than a car. So in conclusion you can see that ebicycles are an ecofriendly, fast, and efficient way to get around in the city.

AUDIO TRACK 1.23 1:38 min

Page 48, Exercise H

Segment 3

JEAN Our last speaker today is Yulia.

YULIA Thank you, Jean. My topic today is electric microcars. Microcars are the smallest cars on the road. By definition, a microcar has seats for only two people. Some cars only have three wheels. Many of them are less than 9 feet long.

In the past, microcars used gasoline, but today, some companies are making them with electric motors. My favorite example is the Tango car.

The Tango is only 8 feet, 6 inches long, or about 257 centimeters, and 39 inches wide. It's the world's narrowest car. Two of them fit in one lane of traffic, and four of them fit in a typical parking space. It has room for two passengers, one behind the other. The battery range is about 100 miles.

The Tango is an example of an electric car that is ecofriendly, easy to park, and fast. The problem is that these cars are very expensive to make—more than $100,000! Today there are only 12 Tangos in the whole world. But as the technology becomes cheaper, electric microcars will definitely become more popular in the future.

AUDIO TRACK 1.24 0:21 min

Page 50, Pronunciation skill: Statement Intonation

MIGUEL My city is in a valley with mountains all around.

JEAN An ebike is basically a regular bike with a motor and a battery.

AUDIO TRACK 1.25 0:53 min

Page 50, Exercise K and Exercise L

1. The Teleférico operates on electricity.
2. The Teleférico has the capacity to carry six-hundred passengers a day.
3. Most ebikes can travel twenty or thirty miles per hour.
4. Ebikes are expensive to buy, but they're cheap to operate.
5. Microcars are the smallest cars on the road.
6. The Tango car has seats for only two people.

AUDIO TRACK 1.26 1:26 min

Part 2, page 53, Exercise D, Vocabulary

a. If you ride a bicycle, be sure to look for **vehicles** before you cross the street.
b. We need three different **remote controls** to operate our television.
c. I have an opinion, but I would like to hear your **perspective** about the plan.
d. It's a simple machine. It has only four **components**, so it's easy to build.
e. One advantage of this bicycle is its **portability**. I can pick it up and carry it on the train.
f. In a car with a gasoline engine, we control **acceleration** by pushing on the gas pedal with our foot.
g. The child sat in the corner by herself and did not **interact** with the other children in the room.
h. I'm not happy with the **performance** of this phone. I expected it to be faster.
i. The driving teacher told me to put my car in **reverse** and look behind me before backing up.
j. Petroleum is not a **sustainable** fuel. We need to start using clean alternatives, such as solar power.

Unit 4

AUDIO TRACK 1.27 2:02 min

Part 1, page 65, Exercise C, Vocabulary

1. Some people really **focus** when they listen to music. They think about the music, and they don't do anything else.
2. Beautiful music **transports** some people. It can inspire their emotions.
3. Some people think live music is more **entertaining** than recorded music. They like to see the musicians play their instruments.
4. Pop music is a big **category**. It includes rock, new wave, and smooth jazz.
5. What is your music-listening style? Do you listen to music while you do other things, or do you just sit and listen?
6. Music in movies can express many different **emotions**. For example, movie music can sound sad, happy, or scary.
7. If you want children to **engage with** music, experts say to take them to concerts when they are very young.
8. According to music experts, a successful pop song is very simple. **Specifically**, it is easy to remember, and it tells a story that is easy to understand.
9. Music helps some people **concentrate**, but other people find it distracting.
10. Nigel Kennedy began his career as a classical violinist, but today he plays other **genres**, too. He recorded a jazz album, *SHHH!*, in 2009.

AUDIO TRACK 1.28 3:27 min

Page 67, Exercise E, Listen for Main Ideas

EMMA Hello out there. Emma Park here, and today we're talking about music, specifically, what are your music-listening habits?

When you think about it, there's music all around us. It's on our phones, it's on our computers. We hear it every time we go to a store. They even play music at my local gas station!

In fact, a recent study showed that most people spend more than 25 hours a week listening to music. That's a lot of listening!

I wondered, with all this listening, *how* are people listening to music these days? Do they just listen, or do they do other things while they're listening?

I was curious, so I went out on the street to find out. I asked people what kind of music they listen to the most, and what they're doing while they're listening to it.

MAN 1 I listen to classical music. I love "the three Bs"—Bach, Beethoven, and Brahms.

Classical music is very emotional for me. It completely transports me. It can make me feel happy, it can make me feel sad. I enjoy feeling all the emotions that classical music expresses.

I really engage with the music, so I don't do anything else when I listen to it. I just sit in a chair and close my eyes and really listen.

WOMAN 1 I listen to rock all day at work. Mostly classic rock, you know, oldies like the Stones, the Beatles.

One reason I like it is I sit at my desk all day, and classic rock helps me focus. It makes me concentrate better on my work, and I think it helps me do a better job.

MAN 2 My favorite music genre is roots music. I specifically like American roots music. It's a big category. It includes the blues, folk, country music… It's music that was born in America. But all cultures have roots music.

I like it because it tells me a lot about the people who created it. Take country music, for example. It tells all kinds of stories, from historical events to sad love affairs.

And I really pay attention to it. I have to drive a lot for my job, and so I listen to roots music while I drive. It's very entertaining. That's the main reason I listen to it.

WOMAN 2 I love jazz. I like it because it's very relaxing for me.

In fact, I have it on all the time. I subscribe to a music streaming service and it's programmed to only play jazz. It's on my phone, on my TV… It's in every room of my apartment. It's like the soundtrack of my life.

EMMA So there you have it. There are a lot of different ways to enjoy music. What's your music listening style?

AUDIO TRACK 1.29 1:10 min
Page 67, Exercise F, Listen for Details

Segment 1
Hello out there. Emma Park here, and today we're talking about music, specifically, what are your music-listening habits?

When you think about it, there's music all around us. It's on our phones, it's on our computers. We hear it every time we go to a store. They even play music at my local gas station!

In fact, a recent study showed that most people spend more than 25 hours a week listening to music. That's a lot of listening!

I wondered, with all this listening, *how* are people listening to music these days? Do they just listen, or do they do other things while they're listening?

I was curious, so I went out on the street to find out. I asked people what kind of music they listen to the most, and what they're doing while they're listening to it.

AUDIO TRACK 1.30 1:09 min
Page 67, Exercise G, Listen for Details

1.

MAN 1 I really engage with the music, so I don't do anything else when I listen to it. I just sit in a chair and close my eyes and really listen.

2.

WOMAN 1 One reason I like it is I sit at my desk all day, and classic rock helps me focus. It makes me concentrate better on my work, and I think it helps me do a better job.

3.

MAN 2 And I really pay attention to it. I have to drive a lot for my job, and so I listen to roots music while I drive. It's very entertaining. That's the main reason I listen to it.

4.

WOMAN 2 I have it on all the time. I subscribe to a music streaming service and it's programmed to only play jazz. It's on my phone, on my TV… It's in every room of my apartment. It's like the soundtrack of my life.

AUDIO TRACK 1.31 1:31 min
Page 68, Exercise H

1.

MAN 1 I listen to classical music. I love "the three Bs"—Bach, Beethoven, and Brahms.

Classical music is very emotional for me. It completely transports me. It can make me feel happy, it can make me feel sad. I enjoy feeling all the emotions that classical music expresses.

2.

WOMAN 1 I listen to rock all day at work. Mostly classic rock, you know, oldies like the Stones, the Beatles.

One reason I like it is I sit at my desk all day, and classic rock helps me focus. It makes me concentrate better on my work, and I think it helps me do a better job.

3.

MAN 2 My favorite music genre is roots music. […]

I like it because it tells me a lot about the people who created it. Take country music, for example. It tells all kinds of stories, from historical events to sad love affairs.

And I really pay attention to it. I have to drive a lot for my job, and so I listen to roots music while I drive. It's very entertaining. That's the main reason I listen to it.

4.

WOMAN 2 I love jazz. I like it because it's very relaxing for me.

AUDIO TRACK 1.32 0:35 min
Page 71, Pronunciation Skill: Contractions with *Be*

what is → what's	who is → who's
we are → we're	he is → he's
it is → it's	there are → there're
she is → she's	they are → they're

AUDIO TRACK 1.33 0:35 min

Page 71, Exercise N

1. There are a lot of good soundtracks.
2. It is my favorite song.
3. Who's your favorite composer?
4. She is a famous songwriter.
5. They're going to a concert.
6. He's a very good guitar player.

AUDIO TRACK 1.34 2:13 min

Part 2, page 73, Exercise C, Vocabulary

a. Beethoven was a classical **composer**. He wrote symphonies and other works of music during the late 18th century and the early 19th century.

b. Daria van den Bercken believes that young children listen to classical music without **prejudice** because they are too young to have any ideas about it yet.

c. One way to reach students who are having trouble understanding a concept is to relate the concept to their everyday lives.

d. Some people are good at playing the piano. I can't **relate** to that because I'm not very musical.

e. Some people don't like jazz music because of its **complexity**. They prefer simpler musical genres such as pop music.

f. Happiness and sadness are **contrasting** emotions. They are opposites.

g. Jazz is a **constant** part of my life. I listen to it all day long.

h. Some rock music is very **energetic**. It sounds very active, and it makes me want to get up and move around.

i. The music of the French composer, Debussy, sounds dreamy and **magical** to me. It has a very charming, enchanting sound.

j. The **elements** of pop music include repetition—repeating sounds—and hooks, which are sounds or words that make listeners pay attention.

Unit 5

AUDIO TRACK 2.2 1:29 min

Part 1, page 85, Exercise C, Vocabulary

a. Grateful people are **aware of** the good things in their lives. They pay attention to these things, and they know how important they are.

b. People who are thankful often have a positive **attitude**. They feel good about life.

c. I am **grateful** for everything you have done for me. Thank you.

d. **Stress** can make you sick. It's better for your health to feel relaxed.

e. People often get more work done if someone appreciates them. For example, workers are often more **productive** when their bosses say "thank you."

f. When you see a kind act, say "thank you." **Recognizing** kindness makes people happy.

g. Gratitude can change people's feelings. It can **affect** them in a good way.

h. **Researchers** such as psychologists study human behavior. They are interested in how our thinking is related to our behavior.

i. When I work hard, no one **acknowledges** it. I wish someone would notice my work.

j. When a person **expresses** thanks, they usually say "thank you."

AUDIO TRACK 2.3 4:14 min

Page 86, Exercise E, Listen for Main Ideas and page 87, Exercise F

PRESENTER Today, we're going to be discussing gratitude. We're going to talk about the *power* of gratitude. So what do you think I mean by gratitude? Yes, you.

MAN 1 Uhhmm...being thankful?

PRESENTER Absolutely! It's a feeling of thankfulness, a feeling of appreciation. It's being aware of the good things in your life, appreciating small things, counting your blessings. Some psychologists call this an "attitude of gratitude." So, does anyone here think they have an "attitude of gratitude"? If so, you must be a happy person.

In fact, there's a connection between being happy and being grateful. This attitude has many benefits. Experts are studying this "attitude of gratitude." They're finding that grateful people have better physical health. They get sick less often and see a doctor less often. Grateful people report that they feel healthier in general. They tend to take better care of themselves. This makes them even healthier. These people also sleep better. In one study, people wrote down what they were grateful for at the end of the day. When they did this, they fell asleep faster and stayed asleep longer. Grateful people have better mental health, too. For example, they have less stress. They're happier and they have stronger social relationships, too.

Gratitude is important at work, as well. Have you ever thought you worked really hard to get a project done, and no one noticed? Studies show that gratitude can lead to happier, more productive workers. For example, Mattel, the toy company, started a program for recognizing and praising employees. As a result, the company was on *Fortune*'s Best Companies to Work For list for several years.

Gratitude can affect the person who receives thanks, too. It can make them more helpful. In one study, people gave a student some help. The student thanked some of the people. He did not thank other people in the study. Then the student asked for more help. The people he thanked gave more help. The people he did not thank gave less help. The researchers had an explanation: It feels good to help. But when someone thanks you, you feel even better. People like to be needed. They feel more valued when someone acknowledges their help. And feeling valued makes people want to be even more helpful. So, gratefulness is important for the person who expresses gratitude, and it's important for the person who receives it.

By now, I imagine many of you are thinking, "How can I get this "attitude of gratitude"? Well, there are a few simple things you can do to develop a sense of gratefulness. Any ideas?

MAN 2 What about this—writing down a few things that you're thankful for each day?

WOMAN 2 What about just saying "thank you" more often?

MAN 3 Or noticing how many kind acts people are always doing, all around you?

WOMAN 3 And thanking them for those actions.

PRESENTER Yes! Those are all great ideas. You're clearly on your way to becoming more grateful! And *I* am very grateful that you all came to my presentation! Thank you! Any questions?

AUDIO TRACK 2.4 0:18 min

Page 86, Listening Skill: Listen for Key Words and Phrases

People who have an "attitude of gratitude" have good physical health.

Grateful people have better mental health, too.

AUDIO TRACK 2.5 1:56 min

Page 87, Exercise G, Listen for Details

Segment 1

PRESENTER Today, we're going to be discussing gratitude. We're going to talk about the *power* of gratitude. So what do you think I mean by gratitude? Yes, you.

MAN 1 Uhhmm…being thankful?

PRESENTER Absolutely! It's a feeling of thankfulness, a feeling of appreciation. It's being aware of the good things in your life, appreciating small things, counting your blessings. Some psychologists call this an "attitude of gratitude." So, does anyone here think they have an "attitude of gratitude"? If so, you must be a happy person.

In fact, there's a connection between being happy and being grateful. This attitude has many benefits. Experts are studying this "attitude of gratitude." They're finding that grateful people have better physical health. They get sick less often and see a doctor less often. Grateful people report that they feel healthier in general. They tend to take better care of themselves. This makes them even healthier. These people also sleep better. In one study, people wrote down what they were grateful for at the end of the day. When they did this, they fell asleep faster and stayed asleep longer. Grateful people have better mental health, too. For example, they have less stress. They're happier and they have stronger social relationships, too.

AUDIO TRACK 2.6 1:32 min

Page 88, Exercise H, Listen for Details

Segment 2

PRESENTER Gratitude is important at work, as well. Have you ever thought you worked really hard to get a project done, and no one noticed? Studies show that gratitude can lead to happier, more productive workers. For example, Mattel, the toy company, started a program for recognizing and praising employees. As a result, the company was on *Fortune*'s Best Companies to Work For list for several years.

Gratitude can affect the person who receives thanks, too. It can make them more helpful. In one study, people gave a student some help. The student thanked some of the people. He did not thank other people in the study. Then the student asked for more help. The people he thanked gave more help. The people he did not thank gave less help. The researchers had an explanation: It feels good to help. But when someone thanks you, you feel even better. People like to be needed. They feel more valued when someone acknowledges their help. And feeling valued makes people want to be even more helpful.

AUDIO TRACK 2.7 1:09 min

Page 88, Exercise I, Listen for Details

Segment 3

PRESENTER So, gratefulness is important for the person who expresses gratitude, and it's important for the person who receives it.

By now, I imagine many of you are thinking, "How can I get this 'attitude of gratitude'? Well, there are a few simple things you can do to develop a sense of gratefulness. Any ideas?

MAN 2 What about this—writing down a few things that you're thankful for each day?

WOMAN 2 What about just saying "Thank you" more often?

MAN 3 Or noticing how many kind acts people are always doing, all around you?

WOMAN 3 And thanking them for those actions.

PRESENTER Yes! Those are all great ideas. You're clearly on your way to becoming more grateful! And *I* am very grateful that you all came to my presentation! Thank you! Any questions?

AUDIO TRACK 2.8 1:02 min

Page 90, Exercise M, Collaborate

PRESENTER So what do you think I mean by gratitude? […] It's a feeling of thankfulness, a feeling of appreciation. It's being aware of the good things in your life, appreciating small things, counting your blessings. Some psychologists call this an "attitude of gratitude."

PRESENTER Gratitude can affect the person who receives thanks, too. It can make them more helpful. In one study, people gave a student some help. The student thanked some of the people. He did not thank other people in the study. Then the student asked for more help. The people he thanked gave more help. The people he did not thank gave less help.

AUDIO TRACK 2.9 0:16 min

Page 91, Pronunciation Skill: Sentence Stress

Today, we're going to be discussing gratitude.

We're going to talk about the power of gratitude.

AUDIO TRACK 2.10 0:48 min

Page 91, Exercise O and page 91, Exercise P

1. So what do you think I mean by gratitude?
2. It's a feeling of thankfulness, a feeling of appreciation.
3. They're finding that grateful people have better physical health.
4. Grateful people have better mental health, too.
5. Gratitude is important at work, as well.
6. Gratitude can affect the person who receives thanks, too.

AUDIO TRACK 2.11 1:53 min

Part 2, page 94, Exercise D, Vocabulary

a. I **attended** a public school. I didn't go to a private school.
b. Krosoczka used his **imagination** to write. He used his original ideas to write many popular children's books.
c. Meeting his lunch lady **inspired** Krosoczka. It gave him the idea to write children's books about a lunch lady hero.

d. Krosoczka wanted to acknowledge lunch ladies for their hard work, so he decided to **create** "School Lunch Hero Day."

e. Krosoczka had an **encounter** with his lunch lady years after he graduated. He didn't expect to meet her, but the meeting changed his life.

f. School lunch **programs** in the United States feed more than 31 million children. The plan to feed children at school started in the 1940s.

g. The lunch ladies at my school **treated** the children well. They behaved in a kind and friendly way.

h. Krosoczka explains how many students at a school in Kentucky **rely on** meals that lunch ladies prepare because they don't get enough food at home.

i. My teacher cried when we thanked him at the end of the school year. We were surprised by his **response**.

j. If you **participate** in class, you will do better in school. Being involved in class activities is the best way to learn.

Unit 6

AUDIO TRACK 2.12 0:34 min

Part 1, page 104, Exercise B, Think Critically, Predict

JUAN Hey Nancy, can I ask you a question?

NANCY Sure, Juan. What is it?

JUAN OK. Um, would you say you're a curious person?

NANCY Am I curious? Oh, absolutely. I'm always looking things up. I probably do about fifty Google searches every day. And I read Wikipedia for fun.

JUAN What about you, David?

AUDIO TRACK 2.13 1:44 min

Page 105, Exercise C, Vocabulary

a. Before you submit your answer, you should be **absolutely** sure it is correct.

b. Yuri didn't go to college, but he has years of **hands-on** experience working as a computer programmer.

c. What was Adam's **reaction** when he found out he was accepted to Harvard? Was he excited?

d. Marci is a serious student. If she's not in class, you can **assume** she's sick.

e. The researcher conducted an experiment with over a hundred volunteer **participants**.

f. Our teacher always **encourages** us to do our best. For example, she writes positive comments on our papers.

g. In the research study, people were asked to taste five kinds of yogurt and **rate** them from 1 to 5 (1 = great, 5 = terrible).

h. The limbic system is the part of the brain that **regulates** our emotions, such as anger, fear, and pleasure.

i. Manuel is always busy because he is **involved in** many social, volunteer, and athletic activities.

j. I read a **fascinating** article about the Trans-Siberian Railway, which travels almost 10,000 kilometers, from Moscow to Vladivostok. I stayed up late last night reading it.

AUDIO TRACK 2.14 3:57 min

Page 106, Exercise E, Listen for Main Ideas

JUAN Hey Nancy, can I ask you a question?

NANCY Sure Juan. What is it?

JUAN OK. Um, would you say you're a curious person?

NANCY Am I curious? Oh, absolutely. I'm always looking things up. I probably do about fifty Google searches every day. And I read Wikipedia for fun.

JUAN What about you, David?

DAVID Yeah, me too. The Internet is a great way to get information. But I really like hands-on learning, too. I remember one time, I was about 8 years old, and I wanted to know what was inside a golf ball. So I went out to the garage and got a saw, and I cut open one of my father's golf balls.

JUAN And? What did you find?

DAVID A lot of thin rubber string, like a really long rubber band, wrapped around a black rubber ball.

NANCY Did you get in trouble for destroying the golf ball?

DAVID No, my parents didn't care about that. But they weren't happy about me using a saw without permission. I'm lucky I still have all my fingers.

JUAN That's funny. What about your teachers? Did they encourage you to be curious?

NANCY Hmm…Well, in my case, some did, and some didn't. My preschool teacher absolutely did. I'll never forget my first science experiment. The teacher gave us paints in different colors and told us to mix them in any way we wanted. That's how I learned that if you mix blue and red you get purple. But then in fourth grade, I asked so many questions that the teacher, in front of the whole class, told me I could only ask one question every hour.

DAVID Oh no! That's awful.

JUAN But that's an unusual reaction, isn't it? I think most teachers really want students to ask questions. Kids learn better when they're curious.

DAVID Well, we assume that, but do we actually know it's true?

JUAN Ha, interesting question! In my psychology class we just read a study about that exact thing. Researchers from the University of California at Davis wanted to find out what happens inside the brain when we're curious.

NANCY How did they study that?

JUAN They designed a very cool experiment. First they asked a group of participants to read a hundred trivia questions, like "What does the word 'dinosaur' mean?" The participants had to rate how curious they were to learn the answer to each question, from 1 to 6. That way, the researchers knew which questions were the most interesting to the participants.

DAVID And? Then what?

JUAN OK, next, the participants reviewed the questions and the answers. At the same time, the researchers used an MRI machine to take pictures of the participants' brains.

NANCY What did the pictures show?

JUAN They showed that when the participants were very curious, the part of the brain that regulates pleasure and reward got excited. It's the same part of the brain that lights up when someone offers us candy or money. That was their first finding.

DAVID That's fascinating.

JUAN Yeah, and also, when the participants were curious, there was more activity in the hippocampus, um, the part of the brain that's involved in creating memories.

NANCY Um-hmm…

JUAN So then, a few days later, the researchers tested the participants on the same trivia questions. Can you guess what they found?

DAVID I guess that it was easier to remember the answers to the questions they were most curious about.

JUAN Exactly. That was the second finding.

NANCY So the lesson is… It feels good to be curious, and when we're curious, we remember stuff more easily.

JUAN Right.

AUDIO TRACK 2.15 2:26 min
Page 107, Exercise F, Listen for Details

Segment 1

JUAN Hey Nancy, can I ask you a question?

NANCY Sure Juan. What is it?

JUAN OK. Um, would you say you're a curious person?

NANCY Am I curious? Oh, absolutely. I'm always looking things up. I probably do about fifty Google searches every day. And I read Wikipedia for fun.

JUAN What about you, David?

DAVID Yeah, me too. The Internet is a great way to get information. But I really like hands-on learning, too. I remember one time, I was about 8 years old, and I wanted to know what was inside a golf ball. So I went out to the garage and got a saw, and I cut open one of my father's golf balls.

JUAN And? What did you find?

DAVID A lot of thin rubber string, like a really long rubber band, wrapped around a black rubber ball.

NANCY Did you get in trouble for destroying the golf ball?

DAVID No, my parents didn't care about that. But they weren't happy about me using a saw without permission. I'm lucky I still have all my fingers.

JUAN That's funny. What about your teachers? Did they encourage you to be curious?

NANCY Hmm… Well, in my case, some did, and some didn't. My preschool teacher absolutely did. I'll never forget my first science experiment. The teacher gave us paints in different colors and told us to mix them in any way we wanted. That's how I learned that if you mix blue and red you get purple. But then in fourth grade, I asked so many questions that the teacher, in front of the whole class, told me I could only ask one question every hour.

DAVID Oh no! That's awful.

JUAN But that's an unusual reaction, isn't it? I think most teachers really want students to ask questions. Kids learn better when they're curious.

DAVID Well, we assume that, but do we actually know it's true?

JUAN Ha, interesting question! In my psychology class we just read a study about that exact thing. Researchers from the University of California at Davis wanted to find out what happens inside the brain when we're curious.

AUDIO TRACK 2.16 1:45 min
Page 107, Exercise G, Listen for Details

Segment 2

NANCY How did they study that?

JUAN They designed a very cool experiment. First they asked a group of participants to read a hundred trivia questions, like "What does the word 'dinosaur' mean?"

The participants had to rate how curious they were to learn the answer to each question, from 1 to 6. That way, the researchers knew which questions were the most interesting to the participants.

DAVID And? Then what?

JUAN OK, next, the participants reviewed the questions and the answers. At the same time, the researchers used an MRI machine to take pictures of the participants' brains.

NANCY What did the pictures show?

JUAN They showed that when the participants were very curious, the part of the brain that regulates pleasure and reward got excited. It's the same part of the brain that lights up when someone offers us candy or money. That was their first finding.

DAVID That's fascinating.

JUAN Yeah, and also, when the participants were curious, there was more activity in the hippocampus, um, the part of the brain that's involved in creating memories.

NANCY Um-hmm…

JUAN So then, a few days later, the researchers tested the participants on the same trivia questions. Can you guess what they found?

DAVID I guess that it was easier to remember the answers to the questions they were most curious about.

JUAN Exactly. That was the second finding.

NANCY So the lesson is… It feels good to be curious, and when we're curious, we remember stuff more easily.

JUAN Right.

AUDIO TRACK 2.17 0:20 min
Page 108, Listening Skill: Make Inferences

NANCY But then in fourth grade, I asked so many questions that the teacher, in front of the whole class, told me I could only ask one question every hour.

AUDIO TRACK 2.18 2:04 min
Page 108, Exercise H, Making Inferences

Segment 1

DAVID I remember one time, I was about 8 years old, and I wanted to know what was inside a golf ball. So I went out to the garage and got a saw, and I cut open one of my father's golf balls.

JUAN And? What did you find?

DAVID A lot of thin rubber string, like a really long rubber band, wrapped around a black rubber ball.

NANCY Did you get in trouble for destroying the golf ball?

DAVID No, my parents didn't care about that. But they weren't happy about me using a saw without permission. I'm lucky I still have all my fingers.

Segment 2

JUAN What about your teachers? Did they encourage you to be curious?

NANCY Hmm… Well, in my case, some did, and some didn't. My preschool teacher absolutely did. I'll never forget my first science experiment. The teacher gave us paints in different colors and told us to mix them in any way we wanted. That's how I learned that if you mix blue and red you get purple. But then in fourth grade, I asked so many questions that the teacher, in front of the whole class, told me I could only ask one question every hour.

DAVID Oh no! That's awful.

Segment 3

NANCY What did the pictures show?

JUAN They showed that when the participants were very curious, the part of the brain that regulates pleasure and reward got excited. It's the same part of the brain that lights up when someone offers us candy or money. That was their first finding.

DAVID That's fascinating.

JUAN Yeah, and also, when the participants were curious, there was more activity in the hippocampus, um, the part of the brain that's involved in creating memories.

AUDIO TRACK 2.19 1:31 min

Page 109, Exercise J

1.

NANCY Did you get in trouble for destroying the golf ball?

DAVID No, my parents didn't care about that. But they weren't happy about me using a saw without permission. I'm lucky I still have all my fingers.

JUAN That's funny.

2.

NANCY But then in fourth grade, I asked so many questions that the teacher, in front of the whole class, told me I could only ask one question every hour.

DAVID Oh no! That's awful.

3.

JUAN In my psychology class we just read a study about that exact thing. Researchers from the University of California at Davis wanted to find out what happens inside the brain when we're curious.

NANCY How did they study that?

4.

NANCY What did the pictures show?

JUAN They showed that when the participants were very curious, the part of the brain that regulates pleasure and reward got excited. It's the same part of the brain that lights up when someone offers us candy or money. That was their first finding.

DAVID That's fascinating.

5.

JUAN Yeah, and also, when the participants were curious, there was more activity in the hippocampus, um, the part of the brain that's involved in creating memories.

NANCY Um-hmm…

AUDIO TRACK 2.20 0:26 min

Page 110, Pronunciation Skill: Intonation in Questions

In yes/no questions, the intonation usually rises at the end:

Would you say you're a curious person?

In Wh- questions, the intonation usually falls at the end:

How did they study that?

AUDIO TRACK 2.21 0:37 min

Page 110, Exercise M

1. **JUAN** Did you get in trouble for destroying the golf ball?
2. **JUAN** What about your teachers?
3. **JUAN** Did they encourage you to be curious?
4. **DAVID** We assume that, but do we actually <u>know</u> it's true?
5. **NANCY** What did the pictures show?
6. **JUAN** Can you guess what they found?

AUDIO TRACK 2.22 1:35 min

Part 2, page 113, Exercise C, Vocabulary

1. The students were watching a **demonstration** in chemistry class when the experiment caught fire.
2. The professor **extended** the art history lecture by adding examples of paintings from more countries.
3. Because a lunar eclipse is a rare **phenomenon**, we spent several days discussing it in science class.
4. Aki practiced her speech out loud several times, so she was able to get up and speak with **confidence** before an audience of 200 people.
5. We were talking about politics when suddenly Marla made a **random** comment about her biology exam.
6. My grandmother is going to have a surgical **procedure** to help her see more clearly.
7. I used a process of **trial and error** until I finally discovered the solution to the problem.
8. After some **reflection**, she decided to sign up for the advanced chemistry class.
9. When I got a C on my research paper, I asked my professor if I could **revise** it and try to get a better grade.
10. All people **deserve** the opportunity for an education, even if they don't have a lot of money.

Unit 7

AUDIO TRACK 2.23 0:22 min

Part 1, page 124, Exercise B, Collaborate

PROFESSOR Today, I'm going to talk about cities. Particularly, things that make them more livable. First of all, what's a "livable" city? Any ideas?

AUDIO TRACK 2.24 2:07 min

Page 125, Exercise C, Vocabulary

a. San Francisco is an **attractive** city. It has beautiful views and good-looking buildings.

b. Cities that have large **public** parks include Mexico City and Moscow. People who live in these cities can use the parks for free.

c. A museum exhibit can **draw** a big crowd of people. For example, over 154,000 people came to the "Titanic" exhibit at the National Mississippi River Museum.

d. Cities that have safe places to walk and exercise help people to **lead** healthier lives.

e. The Walt Disney Concert Hall is a famous **performance center** in Los Angeles, California. You can see orchestras from all over the world there.

f. Many cities provide places for teens to **hang out**. At these places, they can meet friends and participate in activities, such as rock climbing and other sports.

g. An open **sewer** is a danger to public health. In modern cities, underground pipes safely carry waste water away from homes and businesses.

h. Paris-Plage is an area for **recreation** on the River Seine, in Paris, France. It has a sandy beach, a swimming pool, and areas for inline skating, playing volleyball, and other activities.

i. San Francisco **residents** enjoy city life. Most of the people who live there like living in a big city.

j. Cars and **pedestrians** both need to watch out for each other in order to make city streets safe. Walkers and drivers are both responsible for avoiding accidents.

AUDIO TRACK 2.25 3:56 min

Page 126, Exercise E, Listen for Main Ideas

PROFESSOR Today, I'm going to talk about cities. Particularly, things that make them more livable. First of all, what's a "livable" city? Any ideas?

Think for a minute about city life. What are some of the challenges of living in a city?

STUDENT 1 There's crime.

STUDENT 2 They can be dirty and ugly.

STUDENT 3 There is a lot of traffic.

STUDENT 1 They're crowded and noisy.

PROFESSOR Right. These are common problems. Livable cities address these conditions.

The livable city is clean. It's attractive. It's safe. It's easy to get around. It has attractive places to live. It has pleasant, safe public places for people to spend time.

And that's what we're going to look at today. How public space makes cities more livable. Good public spaces draw people together. They also solve other problems of city life. They help people connect with nature and lead healthier lives. Let's take a look at some examples.

This is Factoría Joven. That means "youth factory." It's in Mérida, Spain.

One issue in many cities is the need for places for young people to meet and participate in positive activities.

Factoría Joven solves this problem. On the outside, it's a kind of playground. You can skateboard there. You can go rock climbing. There are walls that people can paint and draw on. There's a performance stage. That's on the outside. There's also indoor space for classes and a computer lab.

It attracts about 150 young people each day. They can learn, get exercise, and just hang out in a safe, urban environment.

So now let's go to Asia. This is Cheonggyecheon Park. Once it was a stream. Then it became an open sewer. After that, a freeway completely covered it. Today, the stream is uncovered. And it's a 7-mile-long recreation area in the heart of Seoul, South Korea.

The stream attracts over 500,000 people each week. Hundreds of events and art festivals take place there each year. And it's open 24 hours a day. It gives Seoul residents a safe, relaxing place to spend time.

And Cheonggyecheon Park addresses a typical city problem, too. Cities can have bad air. But the stream and the surrounding plants improve the air quality.

Okay. Here's an example in Australia.

Many cities want to make public spaces safer for people. A city in new South Wales, Australia, Gosford, solved this problem. It built a footpath—a walkway—near the railway. It provides a safe way for pedestrians and bicyclists to cross the railroad tracks.

But take a look. It's not an ordinary footpath. This footpath glows—that is, it gives off light—in the dark. It's made from phosphorous zinc sulfide. This mineral absorbs light from the sun. The minerals make the path glow for 8-14 hours each day.

It's beautiful, right? People come to the path at night, just to look at it. And the Gosford Glow Footpath doesn't just make the area safer. It also saves money and energy because it provides light without electricity.

So, it's clear that providing public spaces where people can get together and participate in safe and healthy activities is good for a community.

Any questions?

And now, let's talk about…

AUDIO TRACK 2.26 0:47 min

Page 127, Exercise F, Listen for Details

1. One issue in many cities is the need for places for young people to meet and participate in positive activities.

    Factoría Joven solves this problem.

2. And Cheonggyecheon Park addresses a typical city problem, too. Cities can have bad air. But the stream and the surrounding plants improve the air quality.

3. Many cities want to make public spaces safer for people. A city in new South Wales, Australia, Gosford, solved this problem.

AUDIO TRACK 2.27 2:17 min

Page 127, Exercise G, Listen for Details

Segment 1

This is Factoría Joven. That means "youth factory." It's in Mérida, Spain.

One issue in many cities is the need for places for young people to meet and participate in positive activities.

Factoría Joven solves this problem. On the outside, it's a kind of playground. You can skateboard there. You can go rock climbing. There are walls that people can paint and draw on. There's a performance stage. That's on the outside. There's also indoor space for classes and a computer lab.

It attracts about 150 young people each day. They can learn, get exercise, and just hang out in a safe, urban environment.

Segment 2

This is Cheonggyecheon Park. Once it was a stream. Then it became an open sewer. After that, a freeway completely covered it. Today, the stream is uncovered. And it's a 7-mile-long recreation area in the heart of Seoul, South Korea.

The stream attracts over 500,000 people each week. Hundreds of events and art festivals take place there each year. And it's open 24 hours a day. It gives Seoul residents a safe, relaxing place to spend time.

And Cheonggyecheon Park addresses a typical city problem, too. Cities can have bad air. But the stream and the surrounding plants improve the air quality.

Segment 3

Many cities want to make public spaces safer for people. A city in new South Wales, Australia, Gosford, solved this problem. It built a footpath—a walkway—near the railway. It provides a safe way for pedestrians and bicyclists to cross the railroad tracks.

[…]

It's beautiful, right? People come to the path at night, just to look at it. And the Gosford Glow Footpath doesn't just make the area safer. It also saves money and energy because it provides light without electricity.

AUDIO TRACK 2.28 0:15 min

Page 130, Prounciation Skill: Linking

first of all

what's a

some are

AUDIO TRACK 2.29 0:32 min

Page 130, Exercise L

1. These are common problems.
2. It's attractive.
3. It attracts about 150 young people each day.
4. Let's take a look at some examples.
5. They also solve other problems of city life.

AUDIO TRACK 2.30 0:33 min

Page 130, Exercise M

1. It's in Mérida, Spain.
2. That's on the outside.
3. And that's what we're going to look at today.
4. Then it became an open sewer.
5. People come to the path at night, just to look at it.

AUDIO TRACK 2.31 2:14 min

Part 2, page 132, Exercise C, Vocabulary

1. Safdie designs **middle-income** housing projects. They might be too expensive for some people, but you don't have to be rich to live in them.
2. It costs a lot to live in Tokyo and San Francisco. However, Mumbai, India, is one of the most **affordable** cities in the world.
3. People who live in the suburbs have to drive a lot. One way to **sustain** the suburbs is to move businesses into them so people don't have to drive so much.
4. The Outdoor Sculpture Collection at Western Washington University is a public space that is **integrated with** an outdoor art gallery. Students can sit and talk and enjoy art at the same time.
5. We need to look at city living in a new way. For example, we need to **rethink** the way we create housing in crowded cities.
6. Safdie built a unique housing project: Each **unit** is like a house. Residents don't feel like their home is attached to another person's home.
7. The population **density** of large cities gave Safdie an idea: Can we build housing projects that don't feel crowded, even if the city itself is crowded?
8. It costs a lot of money to live in Tokyo. For example, it's **extremely** expensive to buy an apartment there.
9. The architects took an old office building and completely **reconfigured** it. They put shops on the ground floor and apartments on the top floors.
10. A popular **concept** in architecture is creating spaces that help people connect with nature.

Unit 8

AUDIO TRACK 2.32 0:32 min

Part 1, page 144, Exercise B, Collaborate

PROFESSOR Today we're going to talk about change. Specifically, self-change. Making changes in your own life. What kinds of changes do people often want to make in their lives? Any examples?

STUDENT 1 Eat healthier food.

STUDENT 2 Get along better with my family.

STUDENT 3 Be a better student.

STUDENT 4 Get to class on time!

AUDIO TRACK 2.33 1:20 min

Page 145, Exercise D, Vocabulary

1. Cost is an important **factor** to consider when you are choosing a college.
2. If you have a strong **desire** to change your life, you will find a way to do it.
3. The **reward** for studying hard is getting good grades.
4. If you want to **avoid** being late for an appointment, leave earlier.
5. The **punishment** for stealing is jail.
6. A study showed that one **behavior** that many students want to change is staying up very late at night.
7. **Experts** say that students who get enough sleep have better grades.
8. Two **principles** for having a happy life include treating people kindly and having an "attitude of gratitude."
9. It can be difficult to **accomplish** your goals if you don't make a plan.
10. One way to **reinforce** your understanding of a new word is to try to use it five times a day.

AUDIO TRACK 2.34 3:55 min

Page 146, Exercise F, Listen for Main Ideas

PROFESSOR Today we're going to talk about change. Specifically, self-change. Making changes in your own life. What kinds of changes do people often want to make in their lives? Any examples?

STUDENT 1 Eat healthier food.

STUDENT 2 Get along better with my family.

STUDENT 3 Be a better student.

STUDENT 4 Get to class on time!

PROFESSOR Right. So psychologists study how people make changes in their lives. One factor in being able to change is motivation. Motivation is the desire to do things, for example, to change. In order to change, you first have to want to change. You have to be motivated. Psychologists describe two types of motivation: extrinsic and intrinsic.

Extrinsic means coming from outside. People who have extrinsic motivation do things in order to get a reward or to avoid punishment.

So, for example, let's say Sam has extrinsic motivation to start getting to class on time. That means he's doing it because he doesn't want me to give him a bad grade.

VARIOUS STUDENTS

PROFESSOR Now, intrinsic means coming from the inside. People who have intrinsic motivation do things for their own sake. That is, they do a thing because the thing itself is a reward. It's enjoyable. It pleases them. So, if Sam has intrinsic motivation, he'll be on time because he loves to learn and doesn't want to miss anything.

Psychologists say both types of motivation work. But some think that intrinsic motivation is better for making life changes because it's more positive. And as we'll see in a minute, being positive is helpful when making big changes.

So, let's say you want to make a change in your life. How do you go about it? Changing behavior can be hard. But it's not impossible. The good news is that there are strategies that make it easier to change behavior. Experts believe that following certain principles can make change easier. Here are some of their findings:

First, break the new behavior that you want into smaller parts. It's easier to take many small steps instead of one big one. For example, Sam wants to get to places on time. We can break this down into steps. Maybe get to bed earlier. Get up earlier. Load his backpack and put his clothes out the night before. He can list these steps and try to accomplish each one separately. So he can practice going to bed earlier for a few days. That's all he has to do right now. Then when he gets good at that, he starts practicing getting up earlier.

Second, as I just mentioned, be positive. You need to enjoy the process of change. Find pleasure in the new behavior. For example, if Sam starts coming to class on time, he's going to get a head start on the whole day. He'll be on time for everything. This will give him more free time later on. He can look forward to extra time hanging out with friends later.

Finally, pay attention to your process. This helps to reinforce a new behavior. In other words, it helps to make a new behavior a habit. One way to do this is to keep a journal. Write down your plan for change at the start. Then on a daily basis, write about how you are accomplishing the plan.

Well, it looks like our time is up. We'll talk more about this next time.

AUDIO TRACK 2.35 1:43 min

Page 147, Exercise G, Listen for Details

Segment 1

PROFESSOR So psychologists study how people make changes in their lives. One factor in being able to change is motivation. Motivation is the desire to do things, for example, to change. In order to change, you first have to want to change. You have to be motivated. Psychologists describe two types of motivation: extrinsic and intrinsic.

Extrinsic means coming from outside. People who have extrinsic motivation do things in order to get a reward or to avoid punishment.

So, for example, let's say Sam has extrinsic motivation to start getting to class on time. That means he's doing it because he doesn't want me to give him a bad grade.

VARIOUS STUDENTS

PROFESSOR Now, intrinsic means coming from the inside. People who have intrinsic motivation do things for their own sake. That is, they do a thing because the thing itself is a reward. It's enjoyable. It pleases them. So, if Sam has intrinsic motivation, he'll be on time because he loves to learn and doesn't want to miss anything.

Psychologists say both types of motivation work. But some think that intrinsic motivation is better for making life changes because it's more positive. And as we'll see in a minute, being positive is helpful when making big changes.

AUDIO TRACK 2.36 1:56 min

Page 148, Exercise H

Segment 2

Changing behavior can be hard. But it's not impossible. The good news is that there are strategies that make it easier to change behavior. Experts believe that following certain principles can make change easier. Here are some of their findings:

First, break the new behavior that you want into smaller parts. It's easier to take many small steps instead of one big one. For example, Sam wants to get to places on time. We can break this down into steps. Maybe get to bed earlier. Get up earlier. Load his backpack and put his clothes out the night before. He can list these steps and try to accomplish each one separately. So he can practice going to bed earlier for a few days. That's all he has to do right now. Then when he gets good at that, he starts practicing getting up earlier.

Second, as I just mentioned, be positive. You need to enjoy the process of change. Find pleasure in the new behavior. For example, if Sam starts coming to class on time, he's going to get a head start on the whole day. He'll be on time for everything. This will give him more free time later on. He can look forward to extra time hanging out with friends later.

Finally, pay attention to your process. This helps to reinforce a new behavior. In other words, it helps to make a new behavior a habit. One way to do this is to keep a journal. Write down your plan for change at the start. Then on a daily basis, write about how you are accomplishing the plan.

AUDIO TRACK 2.37 0:17 min

Page 150, Pronunciation Skill: Vowels in Unstressed Syllables

a – ware   com – plete   suc – ceed

AUDIO TRACK 2.38 0:38 min

Page 150, Exercise M

1. a – void
2. oc – cur
3. sup – port
4. prob – lem
5. meth – od
6. sys – stem
7. pro – vide
8. com – pare

AUDIO TRACK 2.39 2:00 min

Part 2, page 153, Exercise C, Vocabulary

a. We are all **unique**; no one is exactly like someone else.

b. There was a loud noise when the plane took off. It gave the passengers a feeling of **terror**.

c. If you want to take a trip, don't **postpone** it. You might not be able to do it later.

d. Some people have a sense of **urgency** about making changes when they realize how short life is.

e. She only had one **regret** in life. She didn't finish college.

f. Because of his **ego**, he was not able to recognize his faults, and he had a difficult time getting along with people at work.

g. I **reflected on** the mistakes I made on the test and then decided to change the way I study.

h. To improve your health, try to **eliminate** bad habits like eating junk food and not getting enough exercise

i. It looked like the plane was going to crash, but the pilot landed it safely. It was truly a **miracle**.

j. The speaker told the group, "I **challenge** you to try something new and different each day."

Video Scripts

Unit 1

VIDEO TRACK 1.1 3:46 min

Part 1, page 6, Exercise E, Listen for Main Ideas

HARRY Good afternoon, this is Daily Report and I'm Harry Martinez. Well, today is March 22nd, United Nations World Water Day. And here to talk to us about how we can save this important natural resource is Chandra Cassidy, general manager of the department of water and power. Welcome, Ms. Cassidy.

CHANDRA Thank you very much.

HARRY So first of all, why is it important for everyone, not just people in dry places, to conserve water?

CHANDRA It's important for two reasons. One obvious reason is to save money. Lots of people have very high water bills each month because they use too much water. But more importantly, the world doesn't have enough fresh water. Here are some statistics for your viewers to think about. Water covers 70 percent of the earth, but less than 2 percent is fresh water, water that we can drink. And the world's population is growing. Right now we have almost 7.5 billion people on earth. In thirty years it's going to be 9 billion. Where will we find enough water for all those people?

HARRY Right. So what should people do to save water in their homes? Can you give us some tips?

CHANDRA Sure. Let's start with a really easy one. Don't run the water when you brush your teeth. If you leave the water running, it wastes two and a half gallons of water a minute.

HARRY That's a lot of wasted water. And money.

CHANDRA Yeah, and next, here's another easy one. Take shorter showers. Do you take a shower every day?

HARRY Yes...

CHANDRA How long is your shower, on average?

HARRY I don't know, eight minutes? Ten minutes?

CHANDRA So try to cut your shower time from eight minutes to just five minutes. If you do that, you can save 25 gallons each time you take a shower.

HARRY 25 gallons! That's a lot!

CHANDRA And here's one more tip. Don't eat meat. Or eat less meat. Most people never think about this. It takes a huge amount of water to produce meat. For example, it takes 1,799 gallons of water to produce just one pound of beef.

HARRY Wow, really? Why?

CHANDRA Because you have to feed and take care of the cow for years before you can eat it. And that requires a lot of water.

HARRY I never thought of that before. Anything else?

CHANDRA Yes. Fix leaky faucets. It's crucial to do this because even a small leak can waste a lot of water. In fact, leaks waste more than 3,000 gallons of water a year. That's more than 13 percent of all the water we use.

HARRY Well, thank you for these tips, Chandra. We need to take a break now, but before we go, what message would you like to leave our viewers with?

CHANDRA Well, the main message is that small changes can make a big difference. You can help the environment and save money if you follow these simple suggestions for conserving water.

VIDEO TRACK 1.2 4:15 min

Part 2, page 15, Exercise E, Watch for Main Ideas

JOE SMITH Five hundred seventy-one million two hundred thirty thousand pounds of paper towels are used by Americans every year. If we could—correction, wrong figure—13 billion used every year. If we could reduce the usage of paper towels, one paper towel per person per day, 571,230,000 pounds of paper not used. We can do that.

Now there are all kinds of paper towel dispensers. There's the tri-fold. People typically take two or three. There's the one that cuts it, that you have to tear off. People go one, two, three, four, tear. This much, right? There's the one that cuts itself. People go, one, two, three, four. Or there's the same thing, but recycled paper, you have to get five of those because they're not as absorbent, of course.

The fact is, you can do it all with one towel. The key, two words: This half of the room, your word is "shake." Let's hear it. Shake. Louder.

AUDIENCE Shake.

JS Your word is "fold."

AUDIENCE Fold.

JS Again.

AUDIENCE Fold.

JS Really loud.

AUDIENCE Shake. Fold.

JS Okay. Wet hands. Shake— ne, two, three, four, five, six, seven, eight, nine, 10, 11, 12.
Tri-fold. Fold ... Dry.

(Applause)

AUDIENCE Shake. Fold.

JS Cuts itself. Fold.

AUDIENCE Shake. Fold.

JS Cuts itself. You know the funny thing is, I get my hands drier than people do with three or four, because they can't get in between the cracks. If you think this isn't as good...

AUDIENCE Shake. Fold.

JS Now, there's now a real fancy invention, it's the one where you wave your hand and it kicks it out. It's way too big a towel. Let me tell you a secret. If you're really quick, if you're really quick—and I can prove this—this is half a towel from the dispenser in this building. How? As soon as it starts, you just tear it off. It's smart enough to stop. And you get half a towel.

AUDIENCE Shake. Fold.

JS Now, let's all say it together. Shake. Fold. You will for the rest of your life remember those words every time you pick up a paper towel. And remember, one towel per person for one year—571,230,000 pounds of paper. No small thing. And next year, toilet paper.

(Laughter)

VIDEO TRACK 1.3 2:04 min

Page 16, Exercise G, Watch for Details

Segment 1

Five hundred seventy-one million two hundred thirty thousand pounds of paper towels are used by Americans every year. If we could—correction, wrong figure—13 billion used every year. If we could reduce the usage of paper towels, one paper towel per person per day, 571,230,000 pounds of paper not used. We can do that.

Now there are all kinds of paper towel dispensers. There's the tri-fold. People typically take two or three. There's the one that cuts it, that you have to tear off. People go one, two, three, four, tear. This much, right? There's the one that cuts itself. People go, one, two, three, four. Or there's the same thing, but recycled paper, you have to get five of those because they're not as absorbent, of course.

Segment 2

JS The fact is, you can do it all with one towel. The key, two words: This half of the room, your word is "shake." Let's hear it. Shake. Louder.

AUDIENCE Shake.

JS Your word is "fold."

AUDIENCE Fold.

JS Again.

AUDIENCE Fold.

JS Really loud.

AUDIENCE Shake. Fold.

VIDEO TRACK 1.4 2:02 min

Page 17, Exercise I, Expand your Vocabulary

"Now, there's now a real fancy invention, it's the one where you wave your hand and it **kicks** it **out**."

1. What does **kicks out** mean?
   a. opens automatically
   b. sends out automatically
   c. hits with the foot

"It's **way too big** a towel."

2. What does **way too big** mean?
   a. much larger than needed
   b. a little larger than needed
   c. in the way

"You will **for the rest of your life** remember those words every time you pick up a paper towel."

3. What does **for the rest of your life** mean?
   a. from now until you die
   b. times when you are tired
   c. from your birth until now

"And remember, one towel per person for one year—571,230,000 pounds of paper. **No small thing.**"

4. What does **no small thing** mean?
   a. something small
   b. something important
   c. something you remember

Unit 2

VIDEO TRACK 1.5 3:55 min

Part 1, page 26, Exercise E, Listen for Main Ideas

SHARON Hey Tom! Welcome back! How was your vacation?

TOM It was … awesome.

SHARON Oh yeah? Where did you go?

TOM I went to the Serengeti National Park. I spent ten days on a photo safari.

SHARON Wow! What made you decide to do that?

TOM Well, there were a couple of reasons.

TOM First of all, about six months ago I read an article called something like "Why you should go on a safari to Africa, NOW." The main point was that countries like Kenya and Tanzania rely on tourism to pay for wildlife conservation. And conservation is essential because so many African animals are endangered. For example, there used to be about 65,000 black rhinos in Arica. And now there are only about 4,000 in the whole world. They're almost extinct.

SHARON Really?! What happened to them?

TOM Poaching! People killing them illegally! I decided that if I could help to save rhinos or elephants or any other animals by going on a safari, I was going to do it. That was my main motivation.

SHARON I see. What was the other reason?

TOM Well, you know that I love photography.

SHARON Oh yeah, how many pictures did you take?

TOM About a thousand.

SHARON Oo, can I see them?

TOM Well I only have a few here, but sure. Let's see… OK, here's a typical Serengeti landscape.

SHARON Wait, how big is the Serengeti?

TOM It covers five thousand seven hundred square miles. You can see how flat it is. It's just miles and miles of tall grass, and here and there you see acacia trees, you know, the famous ones that look like umbrellas.

SHARON It's so green.

TOM Yeah, April is the rainy season. It rained every day on my trip.

SHARON Did you travel alone, or did you go with a guide?

TOM I went on a group tour with a professional guide. We traveled in jeeps with seven seats and at night we slept in tents, in a camp.

SHARON That sounds like fun.

TOM Yeah, it was. Here's a picture I took at a drinking hole early one morning.

SHARON I see zebra and… what are these black animals with horns?

TOM They're called wildebeests. They're members of the antelope family. They look kind of scary, don't you think?

SHARON Yeah. Uh, what about the big cats, you know, lions, cheetahs, leopards? Did you see any of those?

TOM No leopards, but lots of lions. Here, look. One afternoon we were driving along and we saw these two female lions lying in the middle of the road, asleep. So our guide stopped the jeep about ten feet away and we just sat there watching them for about fifteen minutes. They never moved.

SHARON Aw, nice picture.

TOM And here's a shot of a female cheetah. She's chasing a baby gazelle, see? The Serengeti has around one thousand five hundred cheetahs. That's the second largest cheetah population in Africa.

SHARON Cheetahs are the fastest land animals, right?

TOM Right.

SHARON That's a great photo. What happened to the gazelle?

TOM The cheetah caught it about 30 seconds after I took this picture.

SHARON Oh no! How did it make you feel to see that?

TOM I … accepted it. See, when you're out there in the park, you realize how everything in nature is connected. Animals like gazelles eat grass and then animals like cheetahs eat gazelles. That's how nature works. It's an endless cycle, and we're just a tiny part of it.

VIDEO TRACK 1.6 3:30 min

Part 2, page 35, Exercise F, Watch for Main Ideas

Everything is interconnected. As a Shinnecock Indian, I was raised to know this. We are a small fishing tribe situated on the southeastern tip of Long Island near the town of Southampton in New York.

When I was a little girl, my grandfather took me to sit outside in the sun on a hot summer day. There were no clouds in the sky. And after a while I began to perspire. And he pointed up to the sky, and he said, "Look, do you see that? That's part of you up there. That's your water that helps to make the cloud that becomes the rain that feeds the plants that feeds the animals."

In my continued exploration of subjects in nature that have the ability to illustrate the interconnection of all life, I started storm chasing in 2008 after my daughter said, "Mom, you should do that."

And so three days later, driving very fast, I found myself stalking a single type of giant cloud called the super cell, capable of producing grapefruit-size hail and spectacular tornadoes, although only two percent actually do. These clouds can grow so big, up to 50 miles wide and reach up to 65,000 feet into the atmosphere. They can grow so big, blocking all daylight, making it very dark and ominous standing under them.

Storm chasing is a very tactile experience. There's a warm, moist wind blowing at your back and the smell of the earth, the wheat, the grass, the charged particles. And then there are the colors in the clouds of hail forming, the greens and the turquoise blues. I've learned to respect the lightning. My hair used to be straight.

(Laughter)

I'm just kidding.

(Laughter)

What really excites me about these storms is their movement, the way they swirl and spin and undulate, with their lava lamp-like mammatus clouds. They become lovely monsters.

When I'm photographing them, I cannot help but remember my grandfather's lesson. As I stand under them, I see not just a cloud, but understand that what I have the privilege to witness is the same forces, the same process in a small-scale version that helped to create our galaxy, our solar system, our sun and even this very planet.

All my relations. Thank you.

VIDEO TRACK 1.7 1:15 min

Page 36, Exercise G, Watch for Details

1. Everything is interconnected.

2. That's your water that helps to make the cloud that becomes the rain that feeds the plants that feeds the animals.

3. And so three days later, driving very fast, I found myself stalking a single type of giant cloud called the super cell, capable of producing grapefruit-size hail and spectacular tornadoes, although only two percent actually do. These clouds can grow so big, up to 50 miles wide and reach up to 65,000 feet into the atmosphere.

VIDEO TRACK 1.8 1:18 min

Page 37, Exercise I, Watch for Details

1. And so three days later, driving very fast, I found myself stalking a single type of giant cloud called the super cell, capable of producing grapefruit-size hail and spectacular tornadoes, although only two percent actually do.

2. Storm chasing is a very tactile experience. There's a warm, moist wind blowing at your back and the smell of the earth, the wheat, the grass, the charged particles. And then there are the colors in the clouds of hail forming, the greens and the turquoise blues. I've learned to respect the lightning. My hair used to be straight.

VIDEO TRACK 1.9 2:44 min

Page 37, Exercise J, Expand your Vocabulary

"When I was a little girl, my grandfather took me to sit outside in the sun on a hot summer day. There were no clouds in the sky. And **after a while** I began to perspire."

1. What does *after a while* mean?
   a. after a few minutes
   b. after a long time
   c. after every time

"And so three days later, driving very fast, I found myself **stalking** a single type of giant cloud called the super cell, capable of producing grapefruit-size hail and spectacular tornadoes, although only two percent actually do."

2. What does *stalking* mean?
   a. thinking about
   b. imagining
   c. following

"I've learned to respect the lightning. My hair used to be straight. [laughter] **I'm** just **kidding**."

3. What does *I'm kidding* mean?
   a. I'm making a joke
   b. I'm talking to children
   c. I'm remembering

"As I stand under them, I see not just a cloud, but understand that what I have the privilege to witness is the same forces, the same process in a **small-scale version** that helped to create our galaxy, our solar system, our sun and even this very planet."

4. What does *small-scale version* mean?
   a. something similar to something else, but smaller
   b. something that weighs less than something else
   c. something that is a new idea

0:37 min

Page 40, Presentation Skill: Use Visual Aids

There were no clouds in the sky. And after a while I began to perspire. And he pointed up to the sky, and he said, "Look, do you see that? That's part of you up there. That's your water that helps to make the cloud that becomes the rain that feeds the plants that feeds the animals."

Unit 3

VIDEO TRACK 1.11 2:09 min
Part 1, page 47, Exercise F, Listen for Details

Segment 1

JEAN Hi everybody. Thanks for attending our panel discussion. Let's start with a little survey. How many of you came to school by private car today? Eleven! Well as you know, a car is not a very ecofriendly method of transportation.

Today we're going to talk about three alternative methods that are ecofriendly, fast, and efficient. Miguel will speak first.

MIGUEL Hi everyone. To begin, I want to tell you about a very unusual method of transportation in La Paz, the biggest city in my country, Bolivia. It is called Mi Teleférico, which means "my cable car." La Paz is in a valley with mountains all around. About 200,000 people live in another small city at the top of the mountain called El Alto. In the past, these people had to travel up and down the mountain by bus or car to get to work. It took a long time, it was dangerous, and all the cars caused a lot of noise, traffic, and pollution.

My city built Mi Teleférico as a solution to these problems. The system opened in 2014 with three lines, and there are plans for six more lines by 2019. Right now it has the capacity to carry 600 passengers per day.

The system has some important benefits for my city. First, a cable car leaves the station every 12 seconds, so it's very convenient. Second, it's fast. It can take passengers from El Alto to La Paz, a distance of about 4 miles, in about 13 minutes. Another plus is that it's cheap; it costs about 40 cents to travel each way. And finally, the system is eco-friendly since it uses electricity.

VIDEO TRACK 1.12 1:22 min
Page 48, Exercise G, Listen for Details

Segment 2

JEAN Thank you, Miguel. Now it's my turn. I'm going to present a type of transportation that's becoming more and more popular all over the world, especially in my country, China—electric bicycles, or ebikes. An ebike is basically a regular bike with a motor and a battery. It's useful, for example, if you're going up a hill.

Most ebikes can easily travel 20 to 30 miles per hour. The battery range is about 18 miles, which is enough for most people to get to and from work. In the United States a basic electric bike costs between a thousand and fifteen hundred dollars. Maybe that's a lot for a bicycle, but after that it's very cheap to operate. It only costs about 15 cents to charge; that's less than a penny per mile. It's three times less expensive than a car. So in conclusion you can see that ebicycles are an ecofriendly, fast, and efficient way to get around in the city.

VIDEO TRACK 1.13 1:39 min
Page 48, Exercise H

Segment 3

JEAN Our last speaker today is Yulia.

YULIA Thank you, Jean. My topic today is electric microcars. Microcars are the smallest cars on the road. By definition, a microcar has seats for only two people. Some cars only have three wheels. Many of them are less than 9 feet long.

In the past, microcars used gasoline, but today, some companies are making them with electric motors. My favorite example is the Tango car.

The Tango is only 8 feet, 6 inches long, or about 257 centimeters, and 39 inches wide. It's the world's narrowest car. Two of them fit in one lane of traffic, and four of them fit in a typical parking space. It has room for two passengers, one behind the other. The battery range is about 100 miles.

The Tango is an example of an electric car that is ecofriendly, easy to park, and fast. The problem is that these cars are very expensive to make—more than $100,000! Today there are only 12 Tangos in the whole world. But as the technology becomes cheaper, electric microcars will definitely become more popular in the future.

VIDEO TRACK 1.14 4:20 min
Part 2, page 55, Exercise F, Watch for Main Ideas

Today I'm going to show you an electric vehicle that weighs less than a bicycle, that you can carry with you anywhere, that you can charge off a normal wall outlet in 15 minutes, and you can run it for 1,000 kilometers on about a dollar of electricity. But when I say the word electric vehicle, people think about vehicles. They think about cars and motorcycles and bicycles, and the vehicles that you use every day. But if you come about it from a different perspective, you can create some more interesting, more novel concepts.

So we built something. I've got some of the pieces in my pocket here. So this is the motor. This motor has enough power to take you up the hills of San Francisco at about 20 miles per hour, about 30 kilometers an hour, and this battery, this battery right here has about six miles of range, or 10 kilometers, which is enough to cover about half of the car trips in the U.S. alone. But the best part about these components is that we bought them at a toy store. These are from remote control airplanes. And the performance of these things has gotten so good that if you think about vehicles a little bit differently, you can really change things.

So today we're going to show you one example of how you can use this. Pay attention to not only how fun this thing is, but also how the portability that comes with this can totally change the way you interact with a city like San Francisco.

(Music) [6 Mile Range] [Top Speed Near 20mph] [Uphill Climbing] [Regenerative Braking]

(Applause) (Cheers)

So we're going to show you what this thing can do. It's really maneuverable. You have a hand-held remote, so you can pretty easily control acceleration, braking, go in reverse if you like, also have braking. It's incredible just how light this thing is. I mean, this is something you can pick up and carry with you anywhere you go.

So I'll leave you with one of the most compelling facts about this technology and these kinds of vehicles. This uses 20 times less energy for every mile or kilometer that you travel than a car, which means not only is this thing fast to charge and really cheap to build, but it also reduces the footprint of your energy use in terms of your transportation. So instead of looking at large amounts of energy needed for each person in this room to get around in a city, now you can look at much smaller amounts and more sustainable transportation.

So next time you think about a vehicle, I hope, like us, you're thinking about something new.

Thank you.

VIDEO TRACK 1.15 1:05 min
Page 56, Exercise G, Watch for Details

Segment 1
Today I'm going to show you an electric vehicle that weighs less than a bicycle, that you can carry with you anywhere, that you can charge off a normal wall outlet in 15 minutes, and you can run it for 1,000 kilometers on about a dollar of electricity. But when I say the word electric vehicle, people think about vehicles. They think about cars and motorcycles and bicycles, and the vehicles that you use every day. But if you come about it from a different perspective, you can create some more interesting, more novel concepts.

VIDEO TRACK 1.16 1:08 min
Page 56, Exercise H, Watch for Details

Segment 2
So we built something. I've got some of the pieces in my pocket here. So this is the motor. This motor has enough power to take you up the hills of San Francisco at about 20 miles per hour, about 30 kilometers an hour, and this battery, this battery right here has about six miles of range, or 10 kilometers, which is enough to cover about half of the car trips in the U.S. alone. But the best part about these components is that we bought them at a toy store. These are from remote control airplanes. And the performance of these things has gotten so good that if you think about vehicles a little bit differently, you can really change things.

VIDEO TRACK 1.17 1:01 min
Page 56, Exercise I, Watch for Details

Segment 3
So I'll leave you with one of the most compelling facts about this technology and these kinds of vehicles. This uses 20 times less energy for every mile or kilometer that you travel than a car, which means not only is this thing fast to charge and really cheap to build, but it also reduces the footprint of your energy use in terms of your transportation. So instead of looking at large amounts of energy needed for each person in this room to get around in a city, now you can look at much smaller amounts and more sustainable transportation.

VIDEO TRACK 1.18 2:46 min
Page 56, Exercise J, Expand your Vocabulary

"Today I'm going to show you an electric vehicle that weighs less than a bicycle, that you can carry with you anywhere, that

you can charge off a normal **wall outlet** in 15 minutes, and you can run it for 1,000 kilometers on about a dollar of electricity."

1. What is a **wall outlet**?
    a. the place you put a plug to get electricity
    b. a large door
    c. the place you rest

"But when I say the word electric vehicle, people think about vehicles. They think about cars and motorcycles and bicycles, and the vehicles that you use every day. But if you come about it from a different perspective, you can create some more interesting, more **novel concepts**."

2. What are **novel concepts**?
    a. ideas about books
    b. new ideas
    c. useful vehicles

"You have a **handheld** remote, so you can pretty easily control acceleration, braking, go in reverse if you like, also have braking."

3. What does **handheld** mean?
    a. designed to fit in your hand
    b. the size of a hand
    c. automatic

"So I'll leave you with one of the most **compelling facts** about this technology and these kinds of vehicles. This uses 20 times less energy for every mile or kilometer that you travel than a car, which means not only is this thing fast to charge and really cheap to build, but it also reduces the footprint of your energy use in terms of your transportation."

4. What are **compelling facts**?
    a. surprising information
    b. very interesting information
    c. unbelievable ideas

Unit 4

VIDEO TRACK 1.19 9:36 min
Part 2, page 75, Exercise E, Watch for Main Ideas

Recently, I flew over a crowd of thousands of people in Brazil playing music by George Frideric Handel. I also drove along the streets of Amsterdam, again playing music by this same composer. Let's take a look.

(Music: George Frideric Handel, "Allegro." Performed by Daria van den Bercken.)

(Video) Daria van den Bercken: I live there on the third floor. (In Dutch) I live there on the corner. I actually live there, around the corner. and you'd be really welcome.

[Man] (In Dutch) Does that sound like fun? Child: (In Dutch) Yes!

[(In Dutch) "Handel house concert"]

(Applause)

Daria van den Bercken: All this was a real magical experience for hundreds of reasons.

Now you may ask, why have I done these things? They're not really typical for a musician's day-to-day life. Well, I did it because I fell in love with the music and I wanted to share it with as many people as possible.

It started a couple of years ago. I was sitting at home on the couch with the flu and browsing the Internet a little, when I found out that Handel had written works for the keyboard. Well, I was surprised. I did not know this. So I downloaded the sheet music and started playing. And what happened next was that I entered this state of pure, unprejudiced amazement. It was an experience of being totally in awe of the music, and I had not felt that in a long time. It might be easier to relate to this when you hear it. The first piece that I played through started like this.

(Music)

Well this sounds very melancholic, doesn't it? And I turned the page and what came next was this.

(Music)

Well, this sounds very energetic, doesn't it? So within a couple of minutes, and the piece isn't even finished yet, I experienced two very contrasting characters: beautiful melancholy and sheer energy. And I consider these two elements to be vital human expressions. And the purity of the music makes you hear it very effectively.

I've given a lot of children's concerts for children of seven and eight years old, and whatever I play, whether it's Bach, Beethoven, even Stockhausen, or some jazzy music, they are open to hear it, really willing to listen, and they are comfortable doing so. And when classes come in with children who are just a few years older, 11, 12, I felt that I sometimes already had trouble in reaching them like that. The complexity of the music does become an issue, and actually the opinions of others—parents, friends, media— they start to count. But the young ones, they don't question their own opinion. They are in this constant state of wonder, and I do firmly believe that we can keep listening like these seven-year-old children, even when growing up. And that is why I have played not only in the concert hall but also on the street, online, in the air: to feel that state of wonder, to truly listen, and to listen without prejudice. And I would like to invite you to do so now. (Music: George Frideric Handel, "Chaconne in G Major." Performed by Daria van den Bercken.)

VIDEO TRACK 1.20 9:45 min
Page 76, Exercise G, Watch for Details

Segment 1
Recently, I flew over a crowd of thousands of people in Brazil playing music by George Frideric Handel. I also drove along the streets of Amsterdam, again playing music by this same composer. Let's take a look.

(Music: George Frideric Handel, "Allegro." Performed by Daria van den Bercken.)

(Video) Daria van den Bercken: I live there on the third floor. (In Dutch) I live there on the corner. I actually live there, around the corner. and you'd be really welcome.

Man: (In Dutch) Does that sound like fun? Child: (In Dutch) Yes!

[(In Dutch) "Handel house concert"]

(Applause)

Daria van den Bercken: All this was a real magical experience for hundreds of reasons.

Now you may ask, why have I done these things? They're not really typical for a musician's day-to-day life. Well, I did it because I fell in love with the music and I wanted to share it with as many people as possible.

It started a couple of years ago. I was sitting at home on the couch with the flu and browsing the Internet a little, when I found out that Handel had written works for the keyboard. Well, I was surprised. I did not know this. So I downloaded the sheet music and started playing. And what happened next was that I entered this state of pure, unprejudiced amazement. It was an experience of being totally in awe of the music, and I had not felt that in a long time. It might be easier to relate to this when you hear it. The first piece that I played through started like this.

(Music)

Well this sounds very melancholic, doesn't it? And I turned the page and what came next was this.

(Music)

Well, this sounds very energetic, doesn't it? So within a couple of minutes, and the piece isn't even finished yet, I experienced two very contrasting characters: beautiful melancholy and sheer energy. And I consider these two elements to be vital human expressions. And the purity of the music makes you hear it very effectively.

Segment 2
I've given a lot of children's concerts for children of seven and eight years old, and whatever I play, whether it's Bach, Beethoven, even Stockhausen, or some jazzy music, they are open to hear it, really willing to listen, and they are comfortable doing so. And when classes come in with children who are just a few years older, 11, 12, I felt that I sometimes already had trouble in reaching them like that. The complexity of the music does become an issue, and actually the opinions of others—parents, friends, media— they start to count. But the young ones, they don't question their own opinion. They are in this constant state of wonder, and I do firmly believe that we can keep listening like these seven-year-old children, even when growing up. And that is why I have played not only in the concert hall but also on the street, online, in the air: to feel that state of wonder, to truly listen, and to listen without prejudice. And I would like to invite you to do so now. (Music: George Frideric Handel, "Chaconne in G Major." Performed by Daria van den Bercken.)

(Applause) Thank you. (Applause)

VIDEO TRACK 1.21 0:40 min
Page 76, Exercise I, Watch for Reasons

Now you may ask, why have I done these things? They're not really typical for a musician's day-to-day life. Well, I did it because I fell in love with the music and I wanted to share it with as many people as possible.

VIDEO TRACK 1.22 2:38 min
Page 77, Exercise J, Expand your Vocabulary

"Now you may ask, why have I done these things? They're not really typical for a musician's **day-to-day** life. Well, I did it because I fell in love with the music and I wanted to share it with as many people as possible."

1. What does **day-to-day** mean?
   a. regular
   b. uninteresting
   c. unusual

"It was an experience of **being** totally **in awe of** the music, and I had not felt that in a long time."

2. What does **being in awe of** mean?
  a. feeling uncomfortable with
  b. feeling amazed by
  c. feeling sad about

"I've given a lot of children's concerts for children of seven and eight years old, and whatever I play, whether it's Bach, Beethoven, even Stockhausen, or some jazzy music, they **are open to** hear it, really willing to listen, and they are comfortable doing so."

3. What does **are open to** mean?
  a. are excited to
  b. are ready to
  c. are not sure how to

"And that is why I have played not only in the concert hall but also on the street, online, in the air: to feel that **state of wonder**, to truly listen, and to listen without prejudice."

4. What is a **state of wonder**?
  a. a condition of feeling amazed
  b. a condition of not knowing
  c. a condition of questioning

VIDEO TRACK 1.23 0:23 min

Page 80, Presentation Skill: Use an Effective Hook

Recently, I flew over a crowd of thousands of people in Brazil playing music by George Frideric Handel

Unit 5

VIDEO TRACK 1.24 4:11 min

Part 1, page 86, Exercise E, Listen for Main Ideas

PRESENTER Today, we're going to be discussing gratitude. We're going to talk about the *power* of gratitude. So what do you think I mean by gratitude? Yes, you.

MAN 1 Uhhmm...being thankful?

PRESENTER Absolutely! It's a feeling of thankfulness, a feeling of appreciation. It's being aware of the good things in your life, appreciating small things, counting your blessings. Some psychologists call this an "attitude of gratitude." So, does anyone here think they have an "attitude of gratitude"? If so, you must be a happy person.

In fact, there's a connection between being happy and being grateful. This attitude has many benefits. Experts are studying this "attitude of gratitude." They're finding that grateful people have better physical health. They get sick less often and see a doctor less often. Grateful people report that they feel healthier in general. They tend to take better care of themselves. This makes them even healthier. These people also sleep better. In one study, people wrote down what they were grateful for at the end of the day. When they did this, they fell asleep faster and stayed asleep longer. Grateful people have better mental health, too. For example, they have less stress. They're happier and they have stronger social relationships, too.

Gratitude is important at work, as well. Have you ever thought you worked really hard to get a project done, and no one noticed? Studies show that gratitude can lead to happier, more productive workers. For example, Mattel, the toy company, started a program for recognizing and praising employees. As a result, the company was on

Fortune's Best Companies to Work For list for several years.

Gratitude can affect the person who receives thanks, too. It can make them more helpful. In one study, people gave a student some help. The student thanked some of the people. He did not thank other people in the study. Then the student asked for more help. The people he thanked gave more help. The people he did not thank gave less help. The researchers had an explanation: It feels good to help. But when someone thanks you, you feel even better. People like to be needed. They feel more valued when someone acknowledges their help. And feeling valued makes people want to be even more helpful. So, gratefulness is important for the person who expresses gratitude, and it's important for the person who receives it.

By now, I imagine many of you are thinking, "How can I get this "attitude of gratitude"? Well, there are a few simple things you can do to develop a sense of gratefulness. Any ideas?

MAN 2 What about this—writing down a few things that you're thankful for each day?

WOMAN 2 What about just saying "thank you" more often?

MAN 3 Or noticing how many kind acts people are always doing, all around you?

WOMAN 3 And thanking them for those actions.

PRESENTER Yes! Those are all great ideas. You're clearly on your way to becoming more grateful! And *I* am very grateful that you all came to my presentation! Thank you! Any questions?

VIDEO TRACK 1.25 5:25 min

Part 2, page 95, Exercise F, Watch for Main Ideas

When my first children's book was published in 2001, I returned to my old elementary school to talk to the students about being an author and an illustrator, and when I was setting up my slide projector in the cafetorium, I looked across the room, and there she was: my old lunch lady. She was still there at the school and she was busily preparing lunches for the day. So I approached her to say hello, and I said, "Hi, Jeannie! How are you?" And she looked at me, and I could tell that she recognized me, but she couldn't quite place me, and she looked at me and she said, "Stephen Krosoczka?" And I was amazed that she knew I was a Krosoczka, but Stephen is my uncle who is 20 years older than I am, and she had been his lunch lady when he was a kid. And she started telling me about her grandkids, and that blew my mind. My lunch lady had grandkids, and therefore kids, and therefore left school at the end of the day? I thought she lived in the cafeteria with the serving spoons. I had never thought about any of that before.

Well, that chance encounter inspired my imagination, and I created the Lunch Lady graphic novel series, a series of comics about a lunch lady who uses her fish stick nunchucks to fight off evil cyborg substitutes, a school bus monster, and mutant mathletes, and the end of every book, they get the bad guy with their hairnet, and they proclaim, "Justice is served!"

(Laughter) (Applause)

And it's been amazing, because the series was so welcomed into the reading lives of children, and they sent me the most amazing letters and cards and artwork. And I would notice as I would visit schools, the lunch staff would be involved in the programming in a very meaningful way. And coast to coast, all of the lunch ladies told me the same thing: "Thank you for making a superhero in our likeness." Because the lunch lady has not been treated very kindly in popular culture over time. But it meant the most to Jeannie. When the books were first published, I invited her to the book launch party, and in front of everyone there, everyone she had fed over the years, I gave her a piece of artwork and some books. And two years after this photo was taken, she passed away, and I attended her wake, and nothing could have prepared me for what I saw there, because next to her casket was this painting, and her husband told me it meant so much to her that I had acknowledged her hard work, I had validated what she did.

And that inspired me to create a day where we could recreate that feeling in cafeterias across the country: School Lunch Hero Day, a day where kids can make creative projects for their lunch staff. And I partnered with the School Nutrition Association, and did you know that a little over 30 million kids participate in school lunch programs every day. That equals up to a little over five billion lunches made every school year.

And the stories of heroism go well beyond just a kid getting a few extra chicken nuggets on their lunch tray. There is Ms. Brenda in California, who keeps a close eye on every student that comes through her line and then reports back to the guidance counselor if anything is amiss. There are the lunch ladies in Kentucky who realized that 67 percent of their students relied on those meals every day, and they were going without food over the summer, so they retrofitted a school bus to create a mobile feeding unit, and they traveled around the neighborhoods feedings 500 kids a day during the summer.

And kids made the most amazing projects. I knew they would. Kids made hamburger cards that were made out of construction paper. They took photos of their lunch lady's head and plastered it onto my cartoon lunch lady and fixed that to a milk carton and presented them with flowers. And they made their own comics, starring the cartoon lunch lady alongside their actual lunch ladies. And they made thank you pizzas, where every kid signed a different topping of a construction paper pizza.

For me, I was so moved by the response that came from the lunch ladies, because one woman said to me, she said, "Before this day, I felt like I was at the end of the planet at this school. I didn't think that anyone noticed us down here." Another woman said to me, "You know, what I got out of this is that what I do is important."

And of course what she does is important. What they all do is important. They're feeding our children every single day, and before a child can learn, their belly needs to be full, and these women and men are working on the front lines to create an educated society.

So I hope that you don't wait for School Lunch Hero Day to say thank you to your lunch staff, and I hope that you remember how powerful a thank you can be. A thank you can change a life. It changes the life of the person who receives it, and it changes the life of the person who expresses it.

Thank you.

(Applause)

VIDEO TRACK 1.26 5:40 min
Page 96, Exercise H, Watch for Details

Segment 1

When my first children's book was published in 2001, I returned to my old elementary school to talk to the students about being an author and an illustrator, and when I was setting up my slide projector in the cafetorium, I looked across the room, and there she was: my old lunch lady. She was still there at the school and she was busily preparing lunches for the day. So I approached her to say hello, and I said, "Hi, Jeannie! How are you?" And she looked at me, and I could tell that she recognized me, but she couldn't quite place me, and she looked at me and she said, "Stephen Krosoczka?" And I was amazed that she knew I was a Krosoczka, but Stephen is my uncle who is 20 years older than I am, and she had been his lunch lady when he was a kid. And she started telling me about her grandkids, and that blew my mind. My lunch lady had grandkids, and therefore kids, and therefore left school at the end of the day? I thought she lived in the cafeteria with the serving spoons. I had never thought about any of that before.

Well, that chance encounter inspired my imagination, and I created the Lunch Lady graphic novel series, a series of comics about a lunch lady who uses her fish stick nunchucks to fight off evil cyborg substitutes, a school bus monster, and mutant mathletes, and the end of every book, they get the bad guy with their hairnet, and they proclaim, "Justice is served!"

Segment 2

And it's been amazing, because the series was so welcomed into the reading lives of children, and they sent me the most amazing letters and cards and artwork. And I would notice as I would visit schools, the lunch staff would be involved in the programming in a very meaningful way. And coast to coast, all of the lunch ladies told me the same thing: "Thank you for making a superhero in our likeness." Because the lunch lady has not been treated very kindly in popular culture over time. But it meant the most to Jeannie. When the books were first published, I invited her to the book launch party, and in front of everyone there, everyone she had fed over the years, I gave her a piece of artwork and some books. And two years after this photo was taken, she passed away, and I attended her wake, and nothing could have prepared me for what I saw there, because next to her casket was this painting, and her husband told me it meant so much to her that I had acknowledged her hard work, I had validated what she did.

And that inspired me to create a day where we could recreate that feeling in cafeterias across the country: School Lunch Hero Day, a day where kids can make creative projects for their lunch staff. And I partnered with the School Nutrition Association, and did you know that a little over 30 million kids participate in school lunch programs every day. That equals up to a little over five billion lunches made every school year.

Segment 3

And the stories of heroism go well beyond just a kid getting a few extra chicken nuggets on their lunch tray. There is Ms. Brenda in California, who keeps a close eye on every student that comes through her line and then reports back to the guidance counselor if anything is amiss. There are the lunch ladies in Kentucky who realized that 67 percent of their students relied on those meals every day, and they were going without food over the summer, so they retrofitted a school bus to create a mobile feeding unit, and they traveled around the neighborhoods feedings 500 kids a day during the summer.

And kids made the most amazing projects. I knew they would. Kids made hamburger cards that were made out of construction paper. They took photos of their lunch lady's head and plastered it onto my cartoon lunch lady and fixed that to a milk carton and presented them with flowers. And they made their own comics, starring the cartoon lunch lady alongside their actual lunch ladies. And they made thank you pizzas, where every kid signed a different topping of a construction paper pizza.

Segment 4

For me, I was so moved by the response that came from the lunch ladies, because one woman said to me, she said, "Before this day, I felt like I was at the end of the planet at this school. I didn't think that anyone noticed us down here." Another woman said to me, "You know, what I got out of this is that what I do is important."

And of course what she does is important. What they all do is important. They're feeding our children every single day, and before a child can learn, their belly needs to be full, and these women and men are working on the front lines to create an educated society.

So I hope that you don't wait for School Lunch Hero Day to say thank you to your lunch staff, and I hope that you remember how powerful a thank you can be. A thank you can change a life. It changes the life of the person who receives it, and it changes the life of the person who expresses it.

Thank you.

(Applause)

VIDEO TRACK 1.27 1:22 min

Page 97, Exercise I, Give Examples

Segment 3

And the stories of heroism go well beyond just a kid getting a few extra chicken nuggets on their lunch tray. There is Ms. Brenda in California, who keeps a close eye on every student that comes through her line and then reports back to the guidance counselor if anything is amiss. There are the lunch ladies in Kentucky who realized that 67 percent of their students relied on those meals every day, and they were going without food over the summer, so they retrofitted a school bus to create a mobile feeding unit, and they traveled around the neighborhoods feedings 500 kids a day during the summer.

And kids made the most amazing projects. I knew they would. Kids made hamburger cards that were made out of construction paper. They took photos of their lunch lady's head and plastered it onto my cartoon lunch lady and fixed that to a milk carton and presented them with flowers. And they made their own comics, starring the cartoon lunch lady alongside their actual lunch ladies. And they made thank you pizzas, where every kid signed a different topping of a construction paper pizza.

VIDEO TRACK 1.28 2:28 min

Page 97, Exercise J, Expand your Vocabulary

"And she started telling me about her grandkids, and that **blew my mind**. My lunch lady had grandkids, and therefore kids, and therefore left school at the end of the day? I

thought she lived in the cafeteria with the serving spoons. I had never thought about any of that before."

1. What does **blew my mind** mean?
   a. surprised me
   b. confused me
   c. made me angry

"For me, I **was** so **moved by** the response that came from the lunch ladies, because one woman said to me, she said, "Before this day, I felt like I was at the end of the planet at this school. I didn't think that anyone noticed us down here." Another woman said to me, "You know, what I got out of this is that what I do is important."

2. What does **was moved by** mean?
   a. felt bored by
   b. had an emotional reaction to
   c. went to a new place

"There is Ms. Brenda in California, who **keeps a close eye on** every student that comes through her line and then reports back to the guidance counselor if anything is amiss."

3. What does **keep a close eye on** mean?
   a. watch carefully
   b. check the eyesight of
   c. understand

"And two years after this photo was taken, she **passed away**, and I attended her wake, and nothing could have prepared me for what I saw there, because next to her casket was this painting, and her husband told me it meant so much to her that I had acknowledged her hard work, I had validated what she did."

4. What does **passed away** mean?
   a. moved
   b. died
   c. said good-bye

Unit 6

VIDEO TRACK 1.29 4:17 min

Part 2, page 116, Exercise F, Watch for Main Ideas

I teach chemistry.

(Explosion)

All right, all right. So more than just explosions, chemistry is everywhere. Have you ever found yourself at a restaurant spacing out just doing this over and over? Some people nodding yes. Recently, I showed this to my students, and I just asked them to try and explain why it happened. The questions and conversations that followed were fascinating.

Check out this video that Maddie from my period three class sent me that evening.

(Clang) (Laughs)

Now obviously, as Maddie's chemistry teacher, I love that she went home and continued to geek out about this kind of ridiculous demonstration that we did in class. But what fascinated me more is that Maddie's curiosity took her to a new level. If you look inside that beaker, you might see a candle. Maddie's using temperature to extend this phenomenon to a new scenario.

You know, questions and curiosity like Maddie's are magnets that draw us towards our teachers, and they transcend all technology or buzzwords in education. But if we place these technologies before student inquiry, we can be robbing ourselves of our greatest tool as teachers: our students' questions. …

… the truth is, I've been teaching for 13 years now, and it took a life-threatening situation to snap me out of 10 years of pseudo-teaching and help me realize that student questions are the seeds of real learning, not some scripted curriculum that gave them tidbits of random information.

In May of 2010, at 35 years old, with a two-year-old at home and my second child on the way, I was diagnosed with a large aneurysm at the base of my thoracic aorta. This led to open-heart surgery. This is the actual real email from my doctor right there. Now, when I got this, I was — press Caps Lock—absolutely freaked out, okay? But I found surprising moments of comfort in the confidence that my surgeon embodied. Where did this guy get this confidence, the audacity of it?

So when I asked him, he told me three things. He said first, his curiosity drove him to ask hard questions about the procedure, about what worked and what didn't work. Second, he embraced, and didn't fear, the messy process of trial and error, the inevitable process of trial and error. And third, through intense reflection, he gathered the information that he needed to design and revise the procedure, and then, with a steady hand, he saved my life.

Now I absorbed a lot from these words of wisdom, and before I went back into the classroom that fall, I wrote down three rules of my own that I bring to my lesson planning still today. Rule number one: Curiosity comes first. Questions can be windows to great instruction, but not the other way around. Rule number two: Embrace the mess. We're all teachers. We know learning is ugly. And rule number three: Practice reflection. What we do is important. It deserves our care, but it also deserves our revision. Can we be the surgeons of our classrooms? As if what we are doing one day will save lives. Our students our worth it.

VIDEO TRACK 1.30 1:10 min
Page 116, Exercise H, Watch for Details

Segment 1
Check out this video that Maddie from my period three class sent me that evening.

(Clang) (Laughs)

Now obviously, as Maddie's chemistry teacher, I love that she went home and continued to geek out about this kind of ridiculous demonstration that we did in class. But what fascinated me more is that Maddie's curiosity took her to a new level. If you look inside that beaker, you might see a candle. Maddie's using temperature to extend this phenomenon to a new scenario.

VIDEO TRACK 1.31 2:23 min
Page 117, Exercise I, Watch and Take Notes

Segment 2
In May of 2010, at 35 years old, with a two-year-old at home and my second child on the way, I was diagnosed with a large aneurysm at the base of my thoracic aorta. This led to open-heart surgery. This is the actual real email from my doctor right there. Now, when I got this, I was—press Caps Lock—absolutely freaked out, okay? But I found surprising moments of comfort in the confidence that my surgeon embodied. Where did this guy get this confidence, the audacity of it?

So when I asked him, he told me three things. He said first, his curiosity drove him to ask hard questions about the procedure, about what worked and what didn't work. Second, he embraced, and didn't fear, the messy process of trial and error, the inevitable process of trial and error. And third, through intense reflection, he gathered the information that he needed to design and revise the procedure, and then, with a steady hand, he saved my life.

Now I absorbed a lot from these words of wisdom, and before I went back into the classroom that fall, I wrote down three rules of my own that I bring to my lesson planning still today. Rule number one: Curiosity comes first. Questions can be windows to great instruction, but not the other way around. Rule number two: Embrace the mess. We're all teachers. We know learning is ugly. And rule number three: Practice reflection. What we do is important. It deserves our care, but it also deserves our revision. Can we be the surgeons of our classrooms? As if what we are doing one day will save lives. Our students our worth it.

VIDEO TRACK 1.32 2:22 min
Page 118, Exercise L, Expand Your Vocabulary

"Have you ever found yourself at a restaurant **spacing out** just doing this over and over?"

1. What does *spacing out* mean?
   a. staring at something and losing track of the things around you
   b. taking a break from work or studying
   c. moving things to make more room

"Now obviously, as Maddie's chemistry teacher, I love that she went home and continued to **geek out** about this kind of ridiculous demonstration that we did in class."

2. What does *geek out* mean?
   a. enjoy something
   b. be excited about a topic that doesn't interest most people
   c. be confused by something

"The truth is, I've been teaching for 13 years now, and it took a life-threatening situation to **snap me out of** 10 years of pseudo-teaching and help me realize that student questions are the seeds of real learning, not some scripted curriculum that gave them tidbits of random information."

3. What does *snap me out of* mean?
   a. make me become interested in
   b. make me surprised by
   c. make me stop

"This is the actual real email from my doctor right there. Now, when I got this, I **was**—press Caps Lock—absolutely **freaked out**, okay?"

4. What does *was freaked out* mean?
   a. felt strange or unusual
   b. was very scared
   c. was in a hurry

VIDEO TRACK 1.33 0:31 min
Page 121, Exercise D

Rule number two: Embrace the mess. We're all teachers. We know learning is ugly.

Unit 7

VIDEO TRACK 1.34 3:53 min

Part 1, page 126, Exercise E, Listen for Main Ideas

PROFESSOR Today, I'm going to talk about cities. Particularly, things that make them more livable. First of all, what's a "livable" city? Any ideas?

Think for a minute about city life. What are some of the challenges of living in a city?

STUDENT 1 There's crime.

STUDENT 2 They can be dirty and ugly.

STUDENT 3 There is a lot of traffic.

STUDENT 1 They're crowded and noisy.

PROFESSOR Right. These are common problems. Livable cities address these conditions.

The livable city is clean. It's attractive. It's safe. It's easy to get around. It has attractive places to live. It has pleasant, safe public places for people to spend time.

And that's what we're going to look at today. How public space makes cities more livable. Good public spaces draw people together. They also solve other problems of city life. They help people connect with nature and lead healthier lives. Let's take a look at some examples.

This is Factoría Joven. That means "youth factory." It's in Mérida, Spain.

One issue in many cities is the need for places for young people to meet and participate in positive activities.

Factoría Joven solves this problem. On the outside, it's a kind of playground. You can skateboard there. You can go rock climbing. There are walls that people can paint and draw on. There's a performance stage. That's on the outside. There's also indoor space for classes and a computer lab.

It attracts about 150 young people each day. They can learn, get exercise, and just hang out in a safe, urban environment.

So now let's go to Asia. This is Cheonggyecheon Park. Once it was a stream. Then it became an open sewer. After that, a freeway completely covered it. Today, the stream is uncovered. And it's a 7-mile-long recreation area in the heart of Seoul, South Korea.

The stream attracts over 500,000 people each week. Hundreds of events and art festivals take place there each year. And it's open 24 hours a day. It gives Seoul residents a safe, relaxing place to spend time.

And Cheonggyecheon Park addresses a typical city problem, too. Cities can have bad air. But the stream and the surrounding plants improve the air quality.

Okay. Here's an example in Australia.

Many cities want to make public spaces safer for people. A city in new South Wales, Australia, Gosford, solved this problem. It built a footpath—a walkway—near the railway. It provides a safe way for pedestrians and bicyclists to cross the railroad tracks.

But take a look. It's not an ordinary footpath. This footpath glows—that is, it gives off light—in the dark. It's made from phosphorous zinc sulfide. This mineral absorbs light from the sun. The minerals make the path glow for 8-14 hours each day.

It's beautiful, right? People come to the path at night, just to look at it. And the Gosford Glow Footpath doesn't just make the area safer. It also saves money and energy because it provides light without electricity.

So, it's clear that providing public spaces where people can get together and participate in safe and healthy activities is good for a community.

Any questions?

And now, let's talk about…

VIDEO TRACK 1.35 2:06 min

Part 2, page 133, Exercise E, Watch for Main Ideas

Segment 1

When, in 1960, still a student, I got a traveling fellowship to study housing in North America. We traveled the country. We saw public housing high-rise buildings in all major cities: New York, Philadelphia. Those who have no choice lived there. And then we traveled from suburb to suburb, and I came back thinking, we've got to reinvent the apartment building. There has to be another way of doing this. We can't sustain suburbs, so let's design a building which gives the qualities of a house to each unit.

Habitat would be all about gardens, contact with nature, streets instead of corridors. We prefabricated it so we would achieve economy, and there it is almost 50 years later. It's a very desirable place to live in. It's now a heritage building, but it did not proliferate.

So a few years ago, we decided to go back and rethink Habitat. Could we make it more affordable? Could we actually achieve this quality of life in the densities that are prevailing today? And we realized, it's basically about light, it's about sun, it's about nature, it's about fractalization. Can we open up the surface of the building so that it has more contact with the exterior?

VIDEO TRACK 1.36 3:24 min

Page 135, Exercise G, Watch for Details

Segment 2

We came up with a number of models: economy models, cheaper to build and more compact; membranes of housing where people could design their own house and create their own gardens. And then we decided to take New York as a test case, and we looked at Lower Manhattan. And we mapped all the building area in Manhattan. On the left is Manhattan today: blue for housing, red for office buildings, retail. On the right, we reconfigured it: the office buildings form the base, and then rising 75 stories above, are apartments. There's a street in the air on the 25th level, a community street. It's permeable. There are gardens and open spaces for the community, almost every unit with its own private garden, and community space all around. And most important, permeable, open. It does not form a wall or an obstruction in the city, and light permeates everywhere.

And in the last two or three years, we've actually been, for the first time, realizing the quality of life of Habitat in real-life projects across Asia. This in Qinhuangdao in China: middle-income housing, where there is a bylaw that every apartment must receive three hours of sunlight. That's measured in the winter solstice. And under construction in Singapore, again middle-income housing, gardens, community streets and parks and so on and so forth. And Colombo.

And I want to touch on one more issue, which is the design of the public realm. A hundred years after we've begun building with tall buildings, we are yet to understand how the tall high-rise building becomes a building block in making a city, in creating the public realm. In Singapore, we had an opportunity: 10 million square feet, extremely high density. Taking the concept of outdoor and indoor, promenades and parks integrated with intense urban life. So they are outdoor spaces and indoor spaces, and you move from one to the other, and there is contact with nature, and most relevantly, at every level of the structure, public gardens and open space: on the roof of the podium, climbing up the towers, and finally on the roof, the sky park, two and a half acres, jogging paths, restaurants, and the world's longest swimming pool. And that's all I can tell you in five minutes.

Thank you.

(Applause)

VIDEO TRACK 1.37 2:30 min

Page 136, Exercise I, Expand Your Vocabulary

So a few years ago, we decided to go back and rethink Habitat. Could we make it more affordable? Could we actually achieve this quality of life in the densities that **are prevailing** today?

1. What does **are prevailing** mean?
  a. are common
  b. are unusual
  c. are useful

"We **came up with** a number of models: economy models, cheaper to build and more compact; membranes of housing where people could design their own house and create their own gardens."

2. What does **came up with** mean?
  a. thought of
  b. bought
  c. built

"This in Qinhuangdao in China: middle-income housing, where there is a bylaw that every apartment must receive three hours of sunlight. That's measured in the winter solstice. And under construction in Singapore, again middle-income housing, gardens, community streets and parks **and so on and so forth**."

3. What does **and so on and so forth** mean?
  a. and other different examples
  b. that's enough
  c. and other similar things

"And I want to **touch on** one more issue, which is the design of the public realm."

4. What does **touch on** mean?
  a. summarize
  b. talk about
  c. get rid of

Unit 8

VIDEO TRACK 1.38 3:56 min

Part 1, page 146, Exercise F, Listen for Main Ideas

PROFESSOR Today we're going to talk about change. Specifically, self-change. Making changes in your own life. What kinds of changes do people often want to make in their lives? Any examples?

STUDENT 1 Eat healthier food.

STUDENT 2 Get along better with my family.

STUDENT 3 Be a better student.

STUDENT 4 Get to class on time!

PROFESSOR Right. So psychologists study how people make changes in their lives. One factor in being able to change is motivation. Motivation is the desire to do things, for example, to change. In order to change, you first have to want to change. You have to be motivated. Psychologists describe two types of motivation: extrinsic and intrinsic.

Extrinsic means coming from outside. People who have extrinsic motivation do things in order to get a reward or to avoid punishment.

So, for example, let's say Sam has extrinsic motivation to start getting to class on time. That means he's doing it because he doesn't want me to give him a bad grade.

VARIOUS STUDENTS

PROFESSOR Now, intrinsic means coming from the inside. People who have intrinsic motivation do things for their own sake. That is, they do a thing because the thing itself is a reward. It's enjoyable. It pleases them. So, if Sam has intrinsic motivation, he'll be on time because he loves to learn and doesn't want to miss anything.

Psychologists say both types of motivation work. But some think that intrinsic motivation is better for making life changes because it's more positive. And as we'll see in a minute, being positive is helpful when making big changes.

So, let's say you want to make a change in your life. How do you go about it? Changing behavior can be hard. But it's not impossible. The good news is that there are strategies that make it easier to change behavior. Experts believe that following certain principles can make change easier. Here are some of their findings:

First, break the new behavior that you want into smaller parts. It's easier to take many small steps instead of one big one. For example, Sam wants to get to places on time. We can break this down into steps. Maybe get to bed earlier. Get up earlier. Load his backpack and put his clothes out the night before. He can list these steps and try to accomplish each one separately. So he can practice going to bed earlier for a few days. That's all he has to do right now. Then when he gets good at that, he starts practicing getting up earlier.

Second, as I just mentioned, be positive. You need to enjoy the process of change. Find pleasure in the new behavior. For example, if Sam starts coming to class on time, he's going to get a head start on the whole day. He'll be on time for everything. This will give him more free time later on. He can look forward to extra time hanging out with friends later.

Finally, pay attention to your process. This helps to reinforce a new behavior. In other words, it helps to make a new behavior a habit. One way to do this is to keep a journal. Write down your plan for change at the start. Then on a daily basis, write about how you are accomplishing the plan.

Well, it looks like our time is up. We'll talk more about this next time.

VIDEO TRACK 1.39 4:54 min

Part 2, page 154, Exercise E, Watch for Main Ideas

Imagine a big explosion as you climb through 3,000 ft. Imagine a plane full of smoke. Imagine an engine going clack, clack, clack. It sounds scary.

Well, I had a unique seat that day. I was sitting in 1D. I was the only one who could talk to the flight attendants. So I looked at them right away, and they said, "No problem. We probably hit some birds." The pilot had already turned the plane around, and we weren't that far. You could see Manhattan. Two minutes later, three things happened at the same time.

The pilot lines up the plane with the Hudson River. That's usually not the route.

(Laughter)

He turns off the engines. Now, imagine being in a plane with no sound. And then he says three words. The most unemotional three words I've ever heard. He says, "Brace for impact." I didn't have to talk to the flight attendant anymore.

(Laughter)

I could see in her eyes, it was terror. Life was over.

Now I want to share with you three things I learned about myself that day. I learned that it all changes in an instant. We have this bucket list, we have these things we want to do in life, and I thought about all the people I wanted to reach out to that I didn't, all the fences I wanted to mend, all the experiences I wanted to have and I never did. I no longer want to postpone anything in life. And that urgency, that purpose, has really changed my life.

The second thing I learned that day — and this is as we clear the George Washington Bridge, which was by not a lot—

(Laughter)

I thought about, wow, I really feel one real regret. I've lived a good life. In my own humanity and mistakes, I've tried to get better at everything I tried. But in my humanity, I also allow my ego to get in. And I regretted the time I wasted on things that did not matter with people that matter. And I thought about my relationship with my wife, with my friends, with people. And after, as I reflected on that, I decided to eliminate negative energy from my life. It's not perfect, but it's a lot better. I've not had a fight with my wife in two years. It feels great. I no longer try to be right; I choose to be happy.

The third thing I learned—and this is as your mental clock starts going, "15, 14, 13." You can see the water coming. I'm saying, "Please blow up." I don't want this thing to break in 20 pieces like you've seen in those documentaries. And as we're coming down, I had a sense of, wow, dying is not scary. It's almost like we've been preparing for it our whole lives. But it was very sad. I didn't want to go; I love my life. And that sadness really framed in one thought, which is, I only wish for one thing. I only wish I could see my kids grow up. About a month later, I was at a performance by my daughter— first-grader, not much artistic talent—

(Laughter)

Yet!

(Laughter)

And I'm bawling, I'm crying, like a little kid. And it made all the sense in the world to me. I realized at that point, by connecting those two dots, that the only thing that matters in my life is being a great dad. Above all, above all, the only goal I have in life is to be a good dad.

I was given the gift of a miracle, of not dying that day. I was given another gift, which was to be able to see into the future and come back and live differently. I challenge you guys that are flying today, imagine the same thing happens on your plane—and please don't—but imagine, and how would you change? What would you get done that you're waiting to get done because you think you'll be here forever? How would you change your relationships and the negative energy in them? And more than anything, are you being the best parent you can?

Thank you.

(Applause)

VIDEO TRACK 1.40 1:39 min

Page 155, Exercise G, Watch for Details

Segment 1

Imagine a big explosion as you climb through 3,000 ft. Imagine a plane full of smoke. Imagine an engine going clack, clack, clack. It sounds scary.

Well, I had a unique seat that day. I was sitting in 1D. I was the only one who could talk to the flight attendants. So I looked at them right away, and they said, "No problem. We probably hit some birds." The pilot had already turned the plane around, and we weren't that far. You could see Manhattan. Two minutes later, three things happened at the same time.

The pilot lines up the plane with the Hudson River. That's usually not the route.

(Laughter)

He turns off the engines. Now, imagine being in a plane with no sound. And then he says three words. The most unemotional three words I've ever heard. He says, "Brace for impact." I didn't have to talk to the flight attendant anymore.

(Laughter)

I could see in her eyes, it was terror. Life was over.

VIDEO TRACK 1.41 3:05 min

Page 155, Exercise H, Listen for Listing Words and page 155, Exercise I, Watch for Details

Segment 2

Now I want to share with you three things I learned about myself that day. I learned that it all changes in an instant. We have this bucket list, we have these things we want to do in life, and I thought about all the people I wanted to reach out to that I didn't, all the fences I wanted to mend, all the experiences I wanted to have and I never did. I no longer want to postpone anything in life. And that urgency, that purpose, has really changed my life.

The second thing I learned that day—and this is as we clear the George Washington Bridge, which was by not a lot—

(Laughter)

I thought about, wow, I really feel one real regret. I've lived a good life. In my own humanity and mistakes, I've tried to get better at everything I tried. But in my humanity, I also allow my ego to get in. And I regretted the time I wasted on things that did not matter with people that matter. And I thought about my relationship with my wife, with my friends, with people. And after, as I reflected on that, I decided to eliminate negative energy from my life. It's not perfect, but it's a lot better. I've not had a fight with my wife in two years. It feels great. I no longer try to be right; I choose to be happy.

The third thing I learned — and this is as your mental clock starts going, "15, 14, 13." You can see the water coming. I'm saying, "Please blow up." I don't want this thing to break in 20 pieces like you've seen in those documentaries. And as we're coming down, I had a sense of, wow, dying is not scary. It's almost like we've been preparing for it our whole lives. But it was very sad. I didn't want to go; I love my life. And that sadness really framed in one thought, which is, I only wish for one thing. I only wish I could see my kids grow up. About a month later, I was at a performance by my daughter—first-grader, not much artistic talent

(Laughter)

Yet!

(Laughter)

And I'm bawling, I'm crying, like a little kid. And it made all the sense in the world to me. I realized at that point, by connecting those two dots, that the only thing that matters in my life is being a great dad. Above all, above all, the only goal I have in life is to be a good dad.

VIDEO TRACK 1.42 0:32 min

Page 156, Exercise J, Watch for Rephrasing

Now I want to share with you three things I learned about myself that day. I learned that it all changes in an instant. We have this bucket list, we have these things we want to do in life, and I thought about all the people I wanted to reach out to that I didn't, all the fences I wanted to mend, all the experiences I wanted to have and I never did.

VIDEO TRACK 1.43 2:04 min

Page 156, Exercise K, Expand Your Vocabulary

"I learned that it all changes **in an instant**."

1. What does **in an instant** mean?
   a. eventually
   b. quickly
   c. easily

"I thought about all the people I wanted **to reach out to** that I didn't, all the fences I wanted to mend, all the experiences I wanted to have and I never did."

2. What does **to reach out to** mean?
   a. say goodbye to
   b. communicate with
   c. touch

"I thought about all the people I wanted to reach out to that I didn't, all the **fences** I wanted **to mend**, all the experiences I wanted to have and I never did."

3. What does **to mend fences** mean?
   a. work I wanted to do
   b. relationships I wanted to fix
   c. new projects I wanted to do

"I realized at that point, by **connecting those** two **dots**, that the only thing that matters in my life is being a great dad."

4. What does **connecting (the) dots** mean?
   a. drawing conclusions from facts
   b. getting people together
   c. reflecting